LOCKPORT

Historic Jewel of the Erie Canal

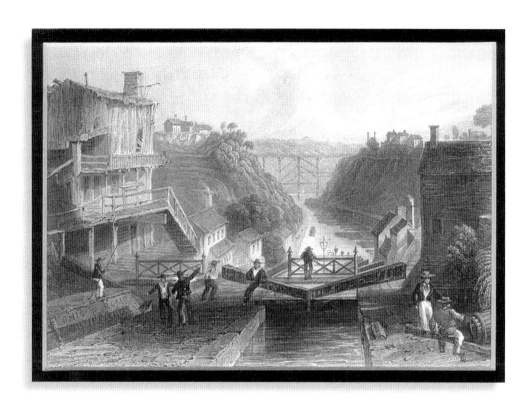

LOCKPORT, ERIE CANAL *BY W. H. BARTLETT. This 1893 view of the Lockport locks from the east is one of prominent illustrator and painter W. H. Bartlett's most famous works in his series on the Erie Canal, reprinted in many American history textbooks.*

LOCKPORT

Historic Jewel of the Erie Canal

KATHLEEN L. RILEY

ARCADIA

Published by Arcadia Publishing,
Charleston SC, Chicago IL, Portsmouth NH, San Francisco CA

Printed in Great Britain.

Library of Congress control number: 2005932603

For all general information contact Arcadia Publishing at:
Telephone 843-853-2070
Fax 843-853-0044
E-Mail sales@arcadiapublishing.com
For customer service and orders:
Toll-Free 1-888-313-2665

Visit us on the Internet at www.arcadiapublishing.com

CONTENTS

Acknowledgments   6

Introduction   8

1. Out of the Wilderness   11

2. Clearing the Forest and Sowing the Seeds of a Town   19

3. Ennobling Work: Lockport's Miracle   31

4. De Witt Clinton's Mission Accomplished   41

5. Curious Manifestations of Bewildering Social Change   54

6. A Christian Enterprise of Vast Proportions   104

7. The Power of Water Creates a Center of Progress   120

8. Hope in the History   140

Bibliography   153
Index   157

ACKNOWLEDGMENTS

The genesis of this book dates back to 1999, when I was appointed a Young Scholar of American Religion and decided to explore my hometown history for the research project. The Local History Room at the Lockport Public Library has summoned me home ever since, particularly the words of former Niagara County Historian Clarence O. Lewis: "There is no hobby more interesting or more useful to posterity than historical research in one's home city or county." This book makes no claim to being a complete history of Lockport; rather, it is one historian's interpretation, an interpretation focused largely on the nineteenth century for two reasons: because that is the part of the past most in danger of being forgotten, and because those were the glory days of Lockport's history.

I have incurred many debts in the course of researching and writing this book. First and foremost, I am grateful to Jim Kempert at Arcadia Publishing for his patience and encouragement. The staff at the Lockport Public Library and the Niagara County Historical Society gave me access to the local records and primary documents essential to this work. The late David Dickinson, Niagara County historian extraordinaire, did the same, and offered words of advice and shared his expertise during the summer months when I was a regular at his office.

The support and assistance of friends and family members sustained me along the way. I owe a special debt of gratitude to my daughter, Emily, for taking some of the recent photographs of Lockport, and for scanning all the pictures for me; I could not have completed the visuals without her assistance. My nephew, Brent Merrill, also took many of the photographs and listened respectfully to my stories of Lockport as I followed him around town. Thanks also to Ann Cavagnaro Fiegl and her family, who were kind enough to share their father/grandfather's collection of historic Lockport slides with me, which helped me frame the material on downtown and the business community. David R. Kinyon, former director of the Lockport/Eastern Niagara County Chamber of Commerce, provided me with a copy of the transcript from the narrative on the "Historic Towpath Trolley" and allowed me to pick his well-informed brain whenever I felt the need.

Finally, I must acknowledge the inspiration provided by Lockport itself. I've learned the truth of the saying that "absence makes the heart grow fonder" since I had to leave my hometown a decade ago to accept a teaching position at Ohio Dominican College. Every time I come home, I appreciate how blessed I was to grow up here. Despite many changes over the years, the small town atmosphere and community spirit has endured and prevailed. Lockport remains a place that remembers and takes care of its own. In one week this past June, the community honored the memory of one of its best-loved citizens and leaders, Barbara McCarthy Ennis, in the annual 5K Memorial Walk that supports her legacy of community service and charitable works. And it welcomed 1971 DeSales High School graduate John Beilein for a visit with great pride—after he coached his University of West Virginia Mountaineers basketball team all the way to the NCAA Elite Eight. Clearly, the welcome signs now posted on the town borders describing Lockport as "A Community That Cares" are not mere expressions of pious sentiment, but offer an accurate assessment of the sprit that still animates Lockport, the "historic jewel of the Erie Canal."

This book is dedicated to my parents, John J. and Patricia Riley, for having the wisdom and good sense to raise their children in a fine place like Lockport.

INTRODUCTION

In *Stars in the Water: The Story of the Erie Canal*, author George Condon focuses a significant amount of his attention on Lockport, a small town in western New York that won fame as the site of the five locks built on the canal in 1825, the engineering marvel of antebellum America: "Lockport, in a real sense, symbolizes the canal. The canal gave the town its being, its name, its prosperity, its look, and its lore."

To set forth the story of Lockport and its illustrious past offers the historian a grand opportunity, for it is a task both novel and challenging. A comprehensive narrative history of Lockport has never been published, though the town and city are certainly worthy of that type of attention. Lockport has always managed to spark interest on the part of those who have written about the Erie Canal, and pictures of the "deep cut" or locks at Lockport are often featured in American history textbooks. Carol Sheriff, author of *The Artificial River: The Erie Canal and the Paradox of Progress, 1817–1862*, discovered that Lockport was the most interesting town on the Erie Canal in the course of her research. Although there has been, and still remains, a good sense of nostalgia in Lockport, a clear perception of its history and how best to preserve it has been lacking over the years—and making the most of the area's potential in this regard has proven to be an elusive dream of politicians and hometown boosters alike.

During the past decade, however, a sense of genuine appreciation for the importance of preserving and promoting Lockport's history has been awakened, and the future looks bright. In the summer of 2000, when the History Channel devoted one of its *Modern Marvels* episodes to the Erie Canal, Lockport was prominently featured in the program, and city officials arranged for a special showing of it at the site of the Lockport Locks and Erie Canal Cruises on Market Street, hopeful of inaugurating a community renaissance based upon history and tourism.

Historian Sheriff commented in that program that the construction of the Erie Canal created New York anew as the Empire State and brought "amazing, unprecedented" changes in its wake, serving as midwife to the birth of so many small towns. The canal spawned an entire industry and way of life, especially true in the case of Lockport—past, present, and future.

The burgeoning field of local history, with its allure for both professionals and amateurs, underscores both the importance and popularity of recovering and preserving the past, and honoring it. Writing the history of one's hometown is a genuine labor of love, but objectivity is called for nonetheless. Small town pride, in both the place and people of Lockport, is a piece in the larger picture of the sense of community that often inspires the historian. In *Rethinking Home: A Case for Writing Local History*, Joseph Amato notes that "local history focuses on the laboratory of change," and "satisfies an innate human desire to be connected to a place—it serves nostalgia." This notion resonates particularly well in Lockport, for its greatest strength is to be found in its history—the glory days of the past and the possibilities that its history presents for a bright future.

Carol Kammen, another local historian based in New York state, shares these sentiments. In her book *On Doing Local History*, she stresses the duty owed to the founders of towns and cities, those "pioneers of civilization." Preserving and transmitting memories, rescuing them from oblivion, is an honorable undertaking, at once "inspirational and instructional," and the lucky historians have found a certain nobility in the nostalgia, striving to "make a contribution that endures." In the case of Lockport, in the opening years of the twenty-first century, this endeavor strives to illustrate the truth of this argument made by historian Kathleen Neils Conzen, that a city is "an organism whose essential history lay in its survival and adaptation in the face of continued challenges."

From its beginnings in the early nineteenth century as the site where "art triumphed over nature," and the "flight of five" locks was an incomparable technological achievement, the town and city of Lockport has faced continued challenges, and succeeded for the most part in meeting them. But the illustrious past has also proven to be a case of the "tough act to follow," and there have been some questions raised over the years about the city's decline as well. Even at a time of great celebration, the 150th anniversary of the Erie Canal in 1975, local son Alexis Muller Jr. wrote a lengthy pamphlet for the Lockport Canal Sesquicentennial Inc. entitled *Looking Back so that we move ahead*. The tone was at once proud yet chastising. He claimed that *Time* magazine had characterized Lockport as "that sleepy little town on the banks of the Erie Canal," suggesting that the charge was "widely resented but never disproved." In some ways, Lockport was an "anachronism"—yet it was also charming and "quaint." Arguing that Lockport had to do more than rest on its laurels if it wanted to remain a vibrant and healthy community, Muller admonished his fellow citizens to study and learn from the mistakes of the past, and "perhaps wake up their sleepy little town."

The years following the anniversary produced some valiant efforts in this direction, as the city tried to capitalize on the past while looking hopefully ahead. Lockport's official seal illustrates the importance of the days when the locks were nationally renowned as the place "where boats sail uphill," and the business/tourist community evokes the folklore of the grand old nicknames for the city of Lockport—the Lock City, the City of Smokeless Power—and, in its advertising brochures: "19th century Marvel, 20th century Heirloom."

For this local daughter/historian, the experience of "faithfulness to home" has indeed proved to be "a compass in a great and shifting sea" (a metaphor evoked in an essay on *The Plight of the Local Historian*). It is a guiding lesson that can be applied to plans to revive the city in the twenty-first century. Those looking to study and preserve the past, and fulfill the city's potential, can find some guidance in the famous words of the proverbial wise man—that "in remembrance resides the secret of redemption." For Lockport's brightest future will most likely be found in remaining true to its status as the Historic Jewel of the Erie Canal, and making the most of its glorious history to ensure its future.

Chapter One

OUT OF THE WILDERNESS

I give you the county of Niagara—the first in the wonders of Nature, and first in the wonders of Art.

—General Lafayette, 1825

The city of Lockport, New York owes its very existence to the building of the Erie Canal. Its fortunes have been inextricably linked to the canal ever since the days of its creation, and the ebb and flow of Lockport's history mirrors that of the artificial river that was destined to turn New York into the Empire State.

Nature: Prelude to Artistic Wonders

Western New York's very early development is a good illustration of the truth of the axiom that geography is destiny, for the region grew around the impressive bodies of water that define the area: the Niagara River and the Great Lakes. Lockport, which would eventually become the seat of Niagara County in the early nineteenth century, has generally been overshadowed by two more famous neighboring cities, Buffalo and Niagara Falls. In terms of both geography and geology, the Falls has dominated the region from the days of its "discovery" by European missionaries in the seventeenth century.

European explorers who visited the New World heard tales of an immense waterfall hidden in the vast recesses of the unknown land. The inhabitants of the Niagara region at the time belonged to the Neuter Indian tribe, later absorbed into the Iroquois nation that became predominant in the environs of New York. One commonly accepted theory about the origins of the word *Niagara*, of Native American origin, says that it stems from the phrase "at the neck," a reference to the Niagara River that joins Lakes Ontario and Erie. In addition to the river, the future Niagara Falls and Lockport were bound together because they were formed by the Niagara escarpment, a massive geologic rock structure transformed by glaciers and erosion over 400 million years ago. It runs in an east-west direction through the center of Niagara County today. Measuring almost 200 feet high in some places, this impressive formation runs from central New York across the Niagara Peninsula into Canada and on to the upper midwest.

This combination of history and geology, water and rock, produced Niagara Falls, one of the great natural wonders of the world. The first written eyewitness testimony to the reality of this natural wonder is attributed to Father Louis Hennepin, a Recollect priest who accompanied LaSalle on his quest for the Mississippi River. His description of what he saw in 1678 is characterized by dread as well as awe and wonder. At once mesmerized and "seized with horror," Hennepin was shaken when he first came upon the great cataract and heard the "dreadful roaring and bellowing of the waters." He wrote that he could not conceive "how it came to pass that four great Lakes . . . should empty themselves at this great Fall, and yet not drown a good part of America." Father Hennepin's exaggerated description of the "prodigious frightful Fall" underscored a dark and mysterious vision of the New World. His commentary on the multitude of rattlesnakes he observed would be echoed by those who first settled Lockport in the nineteenth century, and who soon faced the "impossible" task of digging a canal through the wilderness of primeval forest and rock.

Founding of the Nation: Background to the "Dream" of a Man-Made Waterway

After the successful fight for independence during the Revolutionary War and the establishment of the new nation on a secure footing following the Constitutional Convention, the future of the United States appeared to be one of unlimited possibilities and prospects for growth. According to Carol Sheriff in *The Artificial River,* the prevailing theme in the early development of New York state was progress, and at the center of that vision were plans for constructing a canal to connect the Hudson River to the Great Lakes. This would serve not only the interests of New York but the entire nation, as the canal would serve as a gateway opening up the west to settlement and economic development. The early history of the conception of a canal would be one of fits and starts, plans re-routed and delayed, and the introduction of the element of "paradox," for there were formidable obstacles along the path to progress—physical, economic, and political—and mixed reactions to the canal-building idea.

The notion of a canal running across New York actually dates back prior to the Revolution; there would be no shortage of champions for such a project for the next hundred years, until the goal was accomplished in 1825. As early as the 1720s, Lieutenant Governor Cadwallader Colden offered one of the first proposals to open a waterway by emphasizing the benefits it would bring to the region in terms of increased trade with the Iroquois Indians of western New York. One of Colden's motives was to eliminate the French middlemen from the trade, thereby increasing profits for the English colonists. But the Assembly ignored his advice, and the growing rivalry between the French and the English resulted in the building of Fort Niagara, which would be a scene of conflict during the French and Indian War.

A pioneer in the movement to construct a canal was Gouverneur Morris, member of the First Continental Congress. He envisioned a "peaceful waterway" extending from the Hudson River all the way to Lake Erie. His dreams were bold as he saw the potential of opening up trade between the east and the west, breaking through natural barriers and creating a sense of "national" unity in the making: "The proudest Empire in Europe is but a bubble compared to what America will be, must be, in the course of two centuries . . . perhaps of one."

Following the Revolution, the issue of a canal was revisited. General Philip Schuyler had been instrumental in the plans for some form of navigation system for decades, and in 1792, the New York legislature approved the establishment of two companies. The Western Inland Lock Navigation Company focused on opening "lock navigation from the Hudson River to Seneca Lake," and another concentrated on a route from the Hudson River to Lake Champlain. The common impetus behind these ventures was to supplement the natural waterways, which had "blessed" New York, with man-made creations.

Even as these dreams and schemes were taking shape, the reality of upstate New York, particularly on the western frontier, was wilderness: acres of uninhabited and (at the time) uninhabitable forest, rocks, and gorges that were not amenable to quick settlement. Land speculation and development was the order of the day. In the 1780s and 1790s, Robert Morris and others bought up large tracts of land from Massachusetts and sold much of it to the Holland Land Company. This area would eventually be divided into the eight western counties of New York, and the Holland Land Purchase would serve as the foundation of what would become Niagara County in the early nineteenth century. This area west of the Genesee River attracted the attention of many national figures interested in investments, including the likes of Aaron Burr and Alexander Hamilton. At the close of the eighteenth century, a proposal for building one of the first towns on the Niagara River, Lewiston, was set in motion.

The large scale plans to finance the building of the canal on the part of the New York state legislature looked to Washington and aid from the federal government. President Thomas Jefferson had proposed using surplus federal funds to build roads and canals, so two representatives were sent to make a case for the Erie Canal. But Jefferson's hopes were invested in the Potomac Company, which had been formed in 1785 with George Washington as its president. The company had run out of money, and Jefferson saw the likelihood of success greater in that region of the country. In famous words that ultimately would be proven mistaken and lacking in vision, Jefferson said that the New York canal project was too difficult to be practical at that time: "It is a splendid project and may be executed a century hence . . . you talk of making a canal 350 miles through the wilderness . . . it is little short of madness to think of it at this day!" So, the drive and vision for fulfilling the dream of the grand and glorious Erie would have to come from the locals of New York, specifically the locale of western New York.

"Hercules:" Seer and Promoter of the Canal

Despite Jefferson's failure to appreciate the potential of a canal in upstate New York, the local population, however small, had been able to envision the future benefits that would result from such a historic undertaking. After decades of informal discussion and numerous ideas floated about, three basically different ideas for connecting the Great Lakes to the Hudson River by means of a man-made waterway had emerged by the dawn of the nineteenth century. The first picked up on the old plan of Lieutenant Governor Colden and advocated working westward from Albany, using natural streams and then following the shoreline of Lake Ontario to the Niagara River. Niagara Falls would be bypassed, and a short canal with locks would proceed to Lake Erie. This "Niagara Canal" was actually authorized by the state legislature, but never built.

A second plan was supported by Gouverneur Morris, who would become president of the Canal Commission. It involved construction of an evenly inclined canal from Lake Erie to Albany, with a drop of about one-and-a-half feet per mile. This proposal recognized the formidable physical obstacles that would have to be overcome by building numerous embankments and aqueducts, and the accompanying political difficulties of securing funding.

The third plan, the one eventually followed in constructing the Erie Canal, arose from an unlikely source. In addition to accurately assessing both the route of the canal and the expense, this proposal captured the spirit of confidence and faith in progress that guided the New York visionaries through the difficult years until the successful completion of the canal in 1825, and took note of the guiding hand of "Divine Providence"—or the role of the "Author of nature"—in bringing the vision to fruition. What the canal would come to mean to the New York region, and the nation as a whole, was captured in a series of 14 essays written by "Hercules" in the *Genesee Messenger* from 1807 to 1808. The author was remarkably prescient in outlining both the real and symbolic significance of one of the greatest technological achievements and artistic creations of the American republic.

In reality, Hercules was a down-on-his-luck flour merchant and businessman from western New York, Jesse Hawley, who was serving a 24 month term in a debtors' prison in Canandaigua, New York. Turning this setback around, he concentrated his energies on making a case for the construction of a canal, arguing that it would boost trade, improve communication, and open and expand the west by encouraging emigration along the route he charted. Hawley, "fully persuaded of the practicality of such a canal," seized the opportunity to render himself "useful to society by giving publicity to the suggestion." In keeping with the spirit of post-Revolutionary America, his Hercules essays echoed the style of the *Federalist* papers in laying out a thoughtful, logical, well-argued case for the construction of a canal system in New York—one which would redound favorably for the fortunes of the young Republic. In "Resources on Capital" (no. 7), Hercules offered this synopsis on the multitude of benefits a canal would bring in its wake, echoing the tone of James Madison's *Federalist* no. 10:

> The maxims of politicians are, that rivers unite, mountains divide, governments. . . . the political advantages of opening water communications around and across the intervening mountains, between the great eastern and western sections of the American empire, are, by expediting and familiarizing the intercourse, and by establishing commercial and social connexions between their respective inhabitants, to cultivate genial harmony, and to assimilate their manners in the infancy of our country, which, growing with our maturity, would bind them in their affections to the common government, and secure it from dismemberment.

Starting from the premise that President Jefferson's suggestion that surplus revenues be used for the improvement of canals and roads was "admirable, ingenious and patriotic," Hawley suggested that the improvement that would offer the best and most immediate benefit to the nation was "connecting the waters of *Lake Erie* and those of the *Mohawk* and *Hudson* rivers by means of a canal." Carefully calibrating the mileage and route of such a canal, he set out to provide an answer to the question of whether such a project was feasible, for an artificial waterway was perceived by many as already desirable.

Noting that "sundry canals in Europe" involved a "Herculean task," Hawley said that the doubts voiced about the difficulties inherent in upstate New York "cannot be admitted as insuperable obstacles to the undertaking." It was a project well worth the risks, both physical and financial, for "in a few generations the exhibition of their improvements and the display of their wealth would even scarcely be equaled in the Old World."

His tone of faith and possibility, trusting in the power of the "creator" to guide such a noble undertaking, was characteristic of the American spirit in the early days of the country. Sheriff observed in her monograph on *The Erie Canal and the Paradox of Progress* that in the heyday of the founding of the United States, Americans often ranked the successful founding of their republic as an event "secondary in importance only to the creation of the earth:"

> While the physical world had been the work of God alone, the revolution had been a divinely sanctioned endeavor to perfect the human world. . . . Americans believed that they had been placed on earth to finish God's work in shaping the New World. Their destiny was to perfect the human and physical world. Where God left gaps in the Appalachian Mountains, in other words, He intended humans to create their own rivers.

According to the scenario laid out by Hawley, the people of the state of New York were well up to the challenge. In his "Observations on Canals" piece, he referred to a writer called "Historicus," who opined in a recent New York paper that he "entertained vast ideas of the destinies of these United States. A giant in its infancy, to what point may we not aspire in our maturity." Sharing these aspirations and hopeful expectations of greatness, Hercules wrote that although two thirds of the territory under consideration "remains yet a forest," the natural resources of the new nation were unsurpassed, and the navigable waters of nature comprised a "vast field open to American enterprise." Developing this potential was what he was after in writing his essays, and he responded to the expressed doubts about the possibilities in these words, infused with faith and confidence:

> Why these murmurs? The Creator has done what we can reasonably ask of him. By the falls of Niagara, he has given a head to the waters of Lake Erie sufficient to flow into the channels of the Mohawk and the Hudson, as well as by that of the St. Lawrence. He has only left the finishing stroke to be applied by the hand of art, and it is complete!

Calling upon the citizens of the nation and New York to take up that task as artisans, Hawley's essays served as inspiration for the real undertaking—bringing the work to fruition when the timing was right in the future. His plan was remarkably detailed and accurate in its conception, as he traveled down the proposed route from one end of the state to the other and forecast the "destiny" of several towns: "Albany would be necessitated to cut down her hills and fill her valleys . . . the harbour of Buffalo would exchange her forest trees for a thicket of marine spars." And, summing up "the whole in a sentence, if the project be but a feasible one, no situation on the globe offers such extensive and numerous advantages to inland navigation by a canal, as this!" Clearly, Jesse Hawley forecast a great future for the undeveloped environs of his home, New York—a great drama that would require courage and vision on the part of many other men before the dream would be fulfilled.

Sending out a clarion call for those who would read his essays, he spoke of the "peculiar magnificence" of the country, and suggested that "nature invites Americans to project their plans of internal improvements on her magnificent scale."

Historical Interruption and the Rise of DeWitt Clinton

Writing in 1807–1808, Hercules was a man ahead of his time. But because the president did not share his confidence, the project would have to be funded by the people of New York state alone. The state legislature created the County of Niagara at the western end of the state in 1808 as the population reached 1,200 people; the capital of the new county was located at Buffalo. Working out the practical details of building the canal, however, would be further delayed by the second American war for independence, the War of 1812. Much of the fighting with Great Britain took place in the region Hawley had dreamed about as playing a central role in the continuing drama of American republicanism. Along the border between Canada and New York, the war had devastating effects. Many people left—the population in Niagara County numbered 1,465 in 1810, but had dwindled to 1,276 in 1814. But in the aftermath of the war, new settlers arrived in the area which, phoenix-like, would rise to new heights. For the experience of the war had demonstrated the need for a good waterway in the region, and proved to be a spur to the building of the Erie Canal. With an amazing sense of momentum, the building blocks necessary to realize the dream of Jesse Hawley and many other New Yorkers fell into place starting in 1816.

Many citizens of New York, particularly those in the villages along the proposed route of the canal, began to hold mass meetings demanding that the Canal Commission, established in 1811 before the war, move ahead to make the canal a reality. In New York City, and throughout the state, citizens bombarded the legislature with petitions. The Canal Bill became law, and the Erie Canal—almost exactly matching the detailed proposal offered by Jesse Hawley years ago—was on the verge of becoming an exciting reality. More important, a rising political star, De Witt Clinton, lent his support to the project—a portent of good things to come.

The inspiration and detailed analysis provided by Hawley teamed with Clinton's political power and a fortuitous sense of timing, proved to be a most impressive and successful combination. Sharing a common vision, Clinton had followed Hawley's example in publishing a series of letters signed "Atticus" in the *New York Post* in 1811. These further popularized the notion of a canal, so that when Clinton was elected governor of New York in 1817, he was poised to be the driving force behind the project's take-off. The name DeWitt Clinton was already so closely associated with the Erie Canal that his election can be perceived as a victory for both the man and the idea. When President Madison vetoed the "bonus bill" and the last hopes of federal funding fell through, Governor Clinton had to rally the people of New York to foot the entire bill for the canal on their own. Risking the derision of those who would call his endeavor "Clinton's Ditch" or "Clinton's Folly," he hitched his political star to the Erie Canal, persevering in the face of adversity.

Clinton would not let go of his dream, however many times it was postponed. In 1815, he organized a mass meeting to push the cause forward, and it was a great success. A committee was formed, and charged with the responsibility of drawing up a "Memorial" addressed to the state legislature. This lengthy memorial—"of the Citizens of New York, in favor of a central Navigation between the Great Western Lakes and the tide-waters of the Hudson"—realized its objective, thanks to Clinton's rhetorical skill and marshalling of the facts needed to convince the politicians to act. In a particularly memorable passage, Clinton's rhetoric soared as he made the case that "now is the proper time" to commence the building of the canal:

> Delays are the refuge of weak minds, and to procrastinate on this occasion is to show a culpable inattention to the bounties of nature; a total insensibility to the blessings of Providence, and an inexcusable neglect of the interests of society. If it were intended to advance the view of individuals, or to foment the divisions of party; if it promoted the interests of a few, at the expense of the prosperity of the many; if its benefits were limited as to place, or fugitive as to duration, then indeed it might be received with cold indifference or treated with stern neglect; but the overflowing blessings from this great fountain of public good and national abundance, will be as extensive as our country and as durable as time. . . . It remains for a free state to create a new era in history, and to erect a work more stupendous, more magnificent, and more beneficial than has hitherto been achieved by the human race.

An article in the 1822 *North American Review*, written about midway through the construction of the canal, acknowledged Clinton's important role in making the dream a reality but also noted that Jesse Hawley's 1807 Hercules essays deserved a fair share of the credit. Hawley had functioned as something of a prophet, albeit with dubious honor given his financial predicament. Nevertheless, his work was later hailed in terms of the "boldness of the conception, and the courage of supporting that which was, then, esteemed a wild and extravagant attempt . . . the work of a sagacious, inventive and elevated mind." Men like Clinton and Hawley, who had struggled for years to make their dream a reality, would be appreciated by their contemporaries and future generations for their indomitable will and spirit. Back in 1808, Hawley had made a daring declaration: "New York is destined to be the brightest star in the American galaxy." And once the building of the Erie Canal was underway, this Hercules, recovered from his earlier business failures, would follow his guiding star to an area destined to become famous as the site of the "five tiered locks," built against the odds through the Niagara escarpment. This technological marvel would become the genesis of the town of Lockport, carved out of a vast wilderness in 1821. Not only had he succeeded in making himself useful to society, but his letters had literally put Lockport on the map, so it was fitting that Jesse Hawley would become one of its pioneering residents and most famous sons.

Chapter Two

CLEARING THE FOREST
AND SOWING THE SEEDS OF A TOWN

The site of Lockport! To tell the truth, it has as forbidding an aspect as any spot that has yet been encountered. Ledges of rock, giant forest trees, log and brush heaps, log shanties and rattlesnakes made up a rude landscape that is vividly daguerreotyped in my memory. The contractors were just clearing away an entangled forest that had shaded the deep ravine and excavating the Lock Pit. Drilling and blasting had commenced; there was a clinking of a thousand hand drills; the blasts in the working hours were in almost succession. The atmosphere was murky with the smoke of burning powder. There was a din of battle and yet but the peaceful pursuit of enterprise overcoming the most formidable barrier to the construction of the Erie Canal.

—Diary of Lyman Spalding

The story of the pioneers who first came to the Niagara region of western New York and worked to create a settlement out of this wilderness was initially well-chronicled by one of early Lockport's most prominent citizens. Orsamus Turner's *Pioneer History of the Holland Land Purchase of Western New York,* published in 1850, was written by the publisher and editor of the *Lockport Observatory* newspaper in the flourishing style of a nineteenth century community booster. In the subtitle, Turner indicated that he would cover the highlights of the region's history, from the days of the "Iroquois Indians" to the "origin, progress, and completion of the Erie Canal"—which led to one of the pioneer settlers observing as early as 1821 that Lockport was becoming "a place of no little importance."

In addition to rendering an account of how Lockport came into existence and became the seat of Niagara County, Turner's purpose was to sing the praises of a "small band of adventurers" who brought civilization, however primitive in the early days, to the banks of the Niagara: "Change, progress and improvement will meet us at every step in tracing our local history."

Building the Foundation: Investments of the Holland Land Company

The prologue to Lockport's story begins in 1792, with Robert Morris's sale of land to the Holland Land Company. Surveying the land was the first order of business, dividing the large tract of western New York into lots, sections, and towns. It stretched north to Lake Ontario, west to Lake Erie, and south to the Pennsylvania line. According to

Richard Reed's "Evolutionary History of Niagara County, New York," a reference point had to be struck to the west, which became known as the Transit Line—transformed from a rough trail carved out of the dense forest into the Transit Road or today's state highway 78.

At the dawn of the nineteenth century, the Holland Land Company offered acres of land for sale, and speculation became rampant. Mr. Joseph Ellicott, the principal surveyor of the land, carved out a 6,000 acre section—the Ellicott Reserve or Eleven Mile Woods—on the Ridge Road, near what would grow to become the town of Lockport.

Joshua Wilbur, historian of these rude beginnings and Lockport's early years, compiled information about the hardy individuals who made their way west to lay the foundation for the village that would blossom along with the canal. The first white settlers in this area, west of the towns of Lewiston and Cambria in Niagara County, came to a spot known as Cold Springs, a Native American resort. One of the first structures built in the region was a shelter for the mail carrier, Philip Beach. Charles Wilbur built an inn in addition to a house in 1805, and a village grew up around both Wilbur's establishment and the Wakeman family settlement on Chestnut Ridge, just east of Cold Springs. Sillamon Wakeman arrived from Seneca County in 1809, having spent three weeks cutting his way through the woods, and the arrival of his son Edward in 1810 marked the birth of the first white child at this outpost. In addition, an apple orchard was planted by David Carlton—a harbinger of things to come in terms of the later prominence of the "fruit belt" that comprised much of the rural area around Lockport and gave rise to a thriving industry.

By 1808, with the Ridge Road established, the population reached 1,200, and the citizens petitioned the state legislature to form a new county. On March 11, 1808, the County of Niagara was created. (It would be divided in two with the establishment of Erie County in 1821, with its seat located at Buffalo.) Niagara County's real growth, temporarily set back by the War of 1812, would not take off until the coming of the Erie Canal, as envisioned by Jesse Hawley and brought to fruition by DeWitt Clinton.

Sailing Uphill: Against the Odds

7Even before the state authorized construction of the canal, Clinton spoke to the New York State Historical Society in 1811 on the possibilities and opportunities for greatness that awaited the western portion of the state, challenged yet blessed by nature's design:

> From the Genesee near Rochester to Lewiston on the Niagara, there is a remarkable ridge of elevation of land running along the whole distance . . . this remarkable strip of land would appear as if intended by nature for the purpose of an easy communication. It is, in fact, a stupendous natural turnpike, descending gently on each side . . . but little labor is required to make it the best road in the United States. When the forest between it and the lakes are cleared, the prospects and scenery which will be afforded from a

tour on this route to the cataract of Niagara will surpass all competition for sublimity, beauty, variety and number.

And when the plans to turn the dream of an artificial river across upstate New York became a reality, the stage was set for the emergence of Lockport.

In a *Souvenir Program Commemorating the Lockport Centennial, 1865–1965*, former Niagara County historian Clarence O. Lewis wrote of the genesis of the Lockport story: "Any history of Lockport should begin with the digging of the Erie Canal and the construction of the ten combined locks because our city was born of the canal and received its name from that tremendous engineering feat which proved to the skeptics that boats could 'sail up hill.' " This notion of sailing uphill, calling attention to the engineering marvel of the locks, has often been employed as a motto for Lockport over the years. It is equally applicable to the indomitable spirit of the founding fathers who wedded their fortunes and their futures to the coming of the canal, once the New York state legislature authorized the project in 1816.

Governor Clinton's folly moved a step closer to reality when the route of the Erie Canal was surveyed. Traveling in the west of New York toward Lockport and Buffalo, the surveyors encountered a thick and largely unexplored forest, and another formidable natural obstacle in the rocky formation of the Niagara escarpment. On the occasion of the centennial of the completion of the locks, the 1925 traditional celebration of "Old Home Week" produced a popular historical booklet that noted that "the very early settlers experienced all the trials and hardships that have ever been the penalty of pioneering," demonstrating that Lockport's story was a microcosm of the American conquest of the west. These early settlers had to conquer first the forest, and then the escarpment, in clearing the pathway for the Erie Canal and the town destined to spring up around it.

Growth, Prosperity and Progress in the Air

After the route for the canal was determined and the state legislature authorized the construction to commence, the first ground was broken at Rome, New York on July 4, 1817. Choosing the historic date of the Declaration of Independence was not a coincidence, but a conscious effort to link the fortunes of the Erie Canal with that of the American nation, and the glorious memories associated with a classical empire. Recognizing the daunting task ahead, the members of the state canal commission determined that the work would progress in both directions, toward the east and the west. They hoped that starting at a relatively easy location—Rome, on level ground at the upper limit of navigation on the Mohawk River—would insure some initial success before the real challenges had to be met. Those willing to defy the common wisdom that a series of geographical hurdles along the proposed route might prove insurmountable— rivers, mountains, valleys, and swamps—agreed that the greatest adversary would emerge in the form of the stone escarpment to the west, over 60 feet high. The overall plans for building the canal a distance of 363 miles from Albany to Buffalo would require some means of compensating for the significant elevation discrepancy along the way, for Lake Erie was 568 feet higher than the Hudson River. The solution was found in a series of 83 locks or "water elevators" built to lift boats from one level of the canal to another that were considered to be remarkable feats of scientific ingenuity at the time. By all accounts, the creation of a set of five double locks at Lockport, where boats would have to climb over 60 feet, was little short of miraculous.

Before the successful completion of this engineering marvel, however, the underlying groundwork of the hamlet that grew quickly into a town was laid by the town's founding fathers, who arrived in the environs of Lockport in anticipation of the coming of the canal. They foresaw a promising future, buying up the land and working to plant roots and establish a prosperous community. A retrospective look at the origins of the town, published in 1935 by the Lockport Board of Commerce, observed of these pioneering spirits and their legacy:

> Lockport was founded at a time when fortitude, courage and tenacity were cardinal virtues, at a time when genuine "rugged individualism" meant survival. . . . Lockport's civic progress has been a pageantry of melodrama colored by strong personalities and has ever maintained its pioneering spirit of courage and progress.

The core group of original settlers in Lockport was comprised of a group of approximately 15 men who owned virtually all the land in the area, most of them members of the Society of Friends. These Quakers established the substance and soul of the community, and the prominent names included Esek Brown, Almon Milliard, Reuben Haines, Ashael Smith, Daniel Washburn, and the five Comstock brothers: Nathan, Zeno, Darius, Jared, and John. The Comstocks were developers who followed the lead of the canal surveyors in determining the location of the locks, convinced that this would result in the flowering of a significant community. Theirs was a venture that paid off handsomely, and they served as both the progenitors and beneficiaries of the growth of the village of Lockport.

Zeno and Nathan Comstock had built a dwelling and planted 10 acres of wheat earlier in1816, the first real clearing in the wilderness of forest, and the rudimentary beginnings of a frontier society. Several log houses followed, and the rush of small businesses and mercantile establishments soon started, catering to the needs of the workers on the canal. A very interesting pattern soon emerged, and a multiplicity of taverns and churches would spring up over the next several decades, a strange juxtaposition that would have real social consequences throughout the nineteenth century—particularly with the coming of the Irish immigrants. By 1820, only a few people lived in the nameless village, and the pursuit of progress was just beginning.

The Amazing, Impossible Erie Canal

The task of building occurred on a double track in Lockport: meeting the physical challenge of digging and blasting through the limestone to construct the locks, and laying the foundations for a thriving community. At one and the same time, Lockport came to be recognized for its enterprising spirit—the hustle and bustle of its burgeoning industries—and the engineering marvel and the social tensions that accompanied that rise to prominence and notoriety.

By all accounts, Lockport marked the greatest challenge in terms of the actual construction of the canal—the "deep cut" through three miles of mountainside and limestone. Cheryl Harkness, author of a children's book on the subject, chose the title *The Amazing, Impossible Erie Canal* in an attempt to capture the magnitude of the task undertaken by supporters of Clinton's ditch. The successful completion of the canal was that much sweeter when accomplished against such great odds. It also highlighted the spirit of the "little town that could," and the people who settled there.

Many of those who have chronicled the Lockport story prior to the actual construction of the locks have struck a common theme in their work: colorful personalities and spirits dominated the scene. George Condon's story "Lockport Lore" in his *Stars in the Water* history argues that "its people were unusually endowed in individual brilliance and character, it seemed. It was a town that seemed to specialize in spawning interesting characters the way an Alaskan river spawns salmon." Among those who made noteworthy contributions to the region's early history was a group of standard bearers who arrived at the stage when the hamlet was taking shape. Working together with the first wave of settlers like the enterprising Comstock brothers, these people helped bring about the phenomenal growth that eventually produced Lockport. In the process of telling the story of one of the most enterprising and famous founding fathers, Lyman Spalding, Carol Sheriff noted that in 1821, "only three families lived in the area that would become the town. Six months later, 337 families had moved permanently to the new village." By 1825, when Lockport secured a spot in the national spotlight, the population had skyrocketed to somewhere between 2,500 and 3,700 people—the difficulty of arriving at an accurate count for the historical record says something about the pace of growth. Spalding characterized it as amazing: "What a change in four short years from a state of wilderness."

Tremendous Growth: Dreamers and Entrepreneurs

The core group of men and women who saw the possibilities on the horizon in Lockport worked mightily over the next several years to fulfill their own dreams and the community's potential. It was an eclectic and eccentric cast of characters, ranging from physicians and lawyers to blacksmiths and grocers.

Once the canal commissioners had determined the final route for the canal in western New York, the environs around Lockport and Buffalo served as a magnet, attracting the enterprising spirits who had faith in the future of the area. Some of those pioneers became Lockport's favorite sons and established families still recognized in the city today, whether through their descendents or streets and buildings named after them.

Reuben Haines is a good example of how Lockport became quickly settled by these men, with the work of construction and establishing the basics of a community as their tasks. He was a minister of the Society of Friends, who built a log cabin in 1816. Zeno and John Comstock, Ashael and Daniel Smith, and Webster Thorn followed suit, and their log homes gave an air of permanency to the settlement that had been lacking. Esek Brown's cabin achieved some stature during this stage of amazing growth, for it became the first of several taverns, famous as a gathering place where the founding fathers would eventually choose the name of their community. When the canal construction began, Brown's Tavern, located west of the Transit, became the boarding place and headquarters of the contractors.

In 1818, Jesse Haines, brother of Reuben, arrived. He would be the man responsible for drawing up the first map of the village in 1830. Businesses blossomed, a classic illustration of the adage about "necessity being the mother of invention." Alongside the material side of things, the pioneers recognized the spiritual needs of the settlers by erecting the first churches. In the Lockport Board of Commerce publication of 1935, the central theme of Lockport's history was recognized by recalling that the origin, growth, and development of the city during these formative years were inseparable from that of the canal that ran through it:

> It is those inspired pioneers who envisioned the canal as a great human need, and whose indomitable spirit impelled them to surmount the geological and financial obstacles harassing the construction of this great inland waterway, who are the true founders of Lockport . . . ever since, the growth and development of the city has been synonymous with that of the canal.

The more rudimentary Mountain Road, which connected the Lewiston Road at Cold Springs with neighboring Cambria's Upper Mountain Road, was transformed into Main Street as the village proper took shape and prepared for an influx of canal workers and permanent settlers. The Society of Friends set the spiritual tone of the community from the outset. In 1819, they erected a log structure on a triangular plot bordered by Main, Elm, and Market Streets in the heart of the village. Soon thereafter, the first schoolroom was housed in this community center as well. Zeno Comstock built the first of several sawmills and a grist mill in that same year, and the stage was set for Lockport to take off during the 1820s.

Speculating in land and going after the main chance became the order of the day during these years, as the state contracted for the digging of the canal in western New York. As Orsamus Turner's *History* pointed out, the Comstock brothers, along with Seymour Scovell and Otis Hathaway, had gambled when they first purchased land from the Holland Land Company. Zeno Comstock, "in possession of the most valuable portion of what now constituted the Upper Town," sold his land to his brother Jared and bought at the head of the gulf, anticipating that the canal would follow this route. Instead, Jared was the beneficiary of this bargain, and Zeno pulled up stakes and went west. The canal was destined to be the main arbiter of fortune, then, and the town came to be comprised of a "Lowertown" as well as the Upper Village. A rivalry between these sections would continue into the future, and Lowertown survives to this day.

David Thomas was appointed the chief engineer of the canal construction west of the Genesee River, and Nathan S. Roberts was assigned the task of designing and building the locks. The year 1821 proved to be a watershed year, precipitating major changes in terms of the now bustling community and its inhabitants. Canal contractors placed advertisements in New York City newspapers, seeking men for the hard work of first clearing the forest and then excavating the rocks and digging the canal. Most of these were Irish immigrants, eager to respond to the offer of "twelve dollars a month and found" (room, board, and the occasional reward of a shot of whiskey).

In addition, several of Lockport's most prominent citizens arrived in 1821. Foremost among them was Dr. Isaac Smith, the town's resident physician, and his wife Ednah. One of the few historical records about these early days consists of the memories of "Aunt Ednah." Local folklore remembers her as being known for her benevolent smile and kindness of heart. The Smiths built a home, with a white-washed exterior, at 69 Main Street—the first real house in the heart of the village. It proved to be an excellent vantage point for Ednah to observe the settlement and its myriad activities and characters. Preserved at the Niagara County Historical Society are "Recollections of an Old Settler," which Mrs. Smith dictated to her adopted daughter Mrs. Laura Colton shortly before her death. They provide a treasure trove of eyewitness testimony to the pioneer days of Lockport, and an interpretation of social and cultural mores that has proven valuable to the historian trying to recover the past. Lockport's first historian, Dr. Joshua Wilbur, transcribed the recollections and provided some commentary, and they were first published in the *Lockport Democrat Union* in 1873.

Much of Mrs. Smith's attention was focused on the Irish laborers who had arrived to build the canal, and the chaos that reigned as a result of their presence and their work. Like many early settlers she commented on the rattlesnakes—"the county abounded in them"—and the dangers of the blasting used to remove the rock and limestone obstacles in the canal's proposed path. Daily, one heard warning cries of "look out!"

> Everyone within range flew to a place of shelter. The small stones would rattle down like hail, and were anything but pleasant . . . one stone weighing 18 pounds was thrown over our front yard. Judge [Elias] Ransom, then a young lawyer, had a narrow escape. He had a small office on the south side of Main Street. . . . He was one day sitting in the front room, his chair tilted back, and his feet resting on the table, when crash, came a stone weighing 20 pounds, just within the door, rolled in, hit the legs of the chair and down came the young counselor, in a very undignified manner, and a surprised state of mind at his unexpected fall.

The townspeople, she noted, under "daily siege" from the blasting, hit on the idea of taking cover under the trees. These trees were leaned up against the side of their houses, providing a measure of protection.

Aunt Ednah also provided her own insight into the lives of the Irish, and here she assumed a tone of condescension and haughtiness. The trees provided a practical safeguard, and "the space underneath was utilized by our Irish brethren by being converted into a pig sty or cow home . . . no cholera in those days of impertinent health officials prying into people's domestic arrangements and interfering to prevent their being as dirty as they chose."

The social mixture of Lockport's first generation was a harbinger of trouble and labor violence in the not too distant future. But, as Clarence Lewis wrote in his "Synopsis of the History of Lockport, New York," after the 1,200 laborers reached their destination, "there then began a steady flow of merchants" and other businessmen and shopkeepers "to cater to the needs of this small army." Noteworthy among this group were Deacon Luther Crocker, a blacksmith, and John Jackson, who opened the first bakery on Buffalo Street. Crocker was soon quite successful, as he did much of the iron work on the lock gates, valves, and bridges associated with the canal. Morris Tucker opened the first general store and grocery, and left his own account of his early impressions of the town:

> When I came to Lockport in the summer of 1821, there were some half dozen families residing in unfinished log houses. . . . Esek Brown kept the only tavern in a log house on a rise of ground a little west of the Lutheran Church . . . the land from the head of the locks around the ravine embracing all of Lower Town was a dense forest.
>
> I brought with me from Batavia an old stock of goods which I stored at Esek Brown's until I could build a store. There was no store nearer than Hartland's Corners. When it became known to the women that I had a good tea stored at Brown's, no excuse would answer, have it they would, and I was obliged to open shop. In two or three weeks I moved my goods into a new framed store, an imposing building at the time, twenty-two feet square and a story and a half high. Here for several weeks I had no competition in trade. Soon, however, House and Broughton got their store finished and Libbeus Fish brought goods from Batavia . . . Shepherd and Towner's Shoe Shop, John Jackson's bakery with several small groceries were often named and counted over when recommending our village to some new adventurer, to induce him to buy a village lot. That summer, the rattlesnakes were so numerous that they occasioned much alarm to the villagers.

It was Morris Tucker who had the foresight to christen Lockport "a place of no little importance," an assessment his fellow "adventurers" would surely have agreed with.

Choosing a Name and Continued Progress

Progress was definitely being made, and at breakneck speed. It was time to establish the foundation and governmental structure of a village, and to give it a proper name. There are conflicting stories about the source of the name "Lockport." George L. Lewis, in his "Early History of Lockport & Its Vicinity," relates the tale of Esek Brown's tavern being the inspiration. When Brown returned from Lewiston with a license authorizing him to sell liquor, the agent of the Holland Land Company, Ebenezer Mix, informed him that he could not set up a tavern without giving it a name. Brown did not have a clear idea, so

Mix picked up a board that had served as a door-stop, and wrote "Lockport House" on it in charcoal. He tacked it up on the entrance of the log house, and the name stuck.

A more likely and respectable version of the story centers on the wisdom of the town fathers. In light of the great growth of their little hamlet, and the likelihood of even more, they recognized the importance of determining a suitable name for their beloved community. A group of leading Quaker residents, including the Comstock brothers and Otis Hathaway, gathered at Brown's tavern and came up with several ideas. Quite naturally the set of five locks, designed to overcome the greatest geographic obstacle along the canal route, loomed large in the discussion. Locksborough was suggested by Jesse Haines. Dr. Isaac Smith, however, came up with the simpler Lockport, and final approval was given to that name. It was a fitting choice, for without the locks there would never have been a city carved out of the wilderness.

With a name secured, the future looked even brighter. More enterprising spirits, entrepreneurs willing to invest their time and money, came to seek their fortunes in the bustling village. Jesse Haines had undertaken the job of surveying land and mapping out village lots, and street names were chosen: Walnut, Genesee, Pine, Cottage, Locust, and Canal. To Esek Brown's land were added Niagara, Ontario, Caledonia, and Prospect Streets.

Colonel William Bond was another of the early settlers who arrived in Lockport in 1821. He came from New Hampshire for the express purpose of speculating in land—some writers have referred to him as a bit of a rascal—and purchased a parcel from Esek Brown, which stretched from West Avenue to the present Outwater Park. He was a real wheeler and dealer, and told Brown that he planned to build a glass factory. But he was merely looking to buy up as much land as cheaply as possible in the booming village.

Bond then convinced Brown that the smoke from such a factory would cheapen the value of nearby land, and have an ill effect on neighboring settlers. So Brown agreed to sell the land only if the plans for the glass factory were withdrawn. Bond's plan worked, and he became a wealthy man as a result of his speculation and land grabbing schemes. He built the first brick home in Lockport, which is now on the Historic National Register and comprises part of the Niagara County Historical Society's complex of buildings at 143 Ontario Street. But his fortunes shifted in the 1830s. He lost all his holdings in the Lockport area and sold his home to his sister and her husband, Jesse Hawley—the man who first envisioned the canal in his 1807 Hercules essays. What was once called Bond Street in the north end of town was transformed after Bond went bankrupt, and named Hawley Street to honor this more deserving man.

More businesses mushroomed in Lockport, and the ripple effects of growth were felt everywhere. Clearing the pathway for the canal continued apace, and the transformation was truly remarkable. A "History of Niagara County," published in 1878, contained the following assessment: "At the end of a year a very perceptible change had been wrought, and the infant village had made considerable advance. The forest in the immediate vicinity, mangled and hacked, bore undeniable evidence of the struggle."

Building Amenities on the Foundation

Though Lockport still resembled the frontier in many respects, and the atmosphere of struggle would prevail for several more years, the task of smoothing out the edges of the village was taken up by both the founders and the steady stream of newcomers. Lockport was well on its way to becoming a boom town.

New businesses, churches, and taverns sprang up, and a genuine sense of community flourished. The Lockport Hotel was built on the west bank of the canal. Samuel Jennings, proprietor, advertised his "convenient building for a public house" by "promising to spare no pains to afford comfort and satisfaction" to customers willing to favor him with their company. Almon H. Millard was appointed to the office of sheriff, and also established the first cemetery in Lockport by donating an acre of land for that purpose. Asabel Jackson became the first village clerk. The basic amenities of a more civilized village were being established, which in turn attracted more business. Then Lockport's stock rose dramatically in 1822 when it was named the seat of Niagara County.

When Lockport was on the rise, a real rivalry with the neighboring town of Lewiston developed over the honor of being named the county seat. The ambitious men of Lockport worked to give every advantage to their village, and devised a plan. Aunt Ednah provided these details of the "amusing incident" that helped resolve the matter in favor of Lockport:

> Lewiston claimed the buildings [the Court House and County Building] as being the largest and oldest village in the county . . . Lockport asserted the right as being nearer the geographical center and from the location of the canal and the locks, as likely to be the business and commercial center . . . the Lewistonians had the advantage in possessing a newspaper, by which they could send out their side of the question all over the County . . . some of the more enterprising Lockport citizens met and appointed a committee, consisting of Dr. Isaac Smith and Otis Hathaway, to go over to Lewiston. . . . They left one afternoon with two lumber wagons, reached Lewiston just after dark, found the printer, bought the press, and engaged him to go back with them and run it. [They] were back in Lockport before morning the next day, and by noon the same day had a paper out on their side, with fiery and convincing articles . . . they sent some over to Lewiston that night, which was the first intimation many of the inhabitants had that they were minus a paper. When the Commissioners finally decided in favor of Lockport, I well remember Dr. Smith, who was wildly enthusiastic and public spirited, mount his sorrel Indian pony at the head of Main St. . . . take the newspaper containing the intelligence of their decision in favor of Lockport in one hand, and swinging his hat in the other, spur his horse on a gallop the whole length of Main Street, across "Big Bridge" to the Washington House, shouting the glad news at the top of his voice.

Orsamus Turner, a publisher with a keen sense of history, purchased the paper and became its editor later that year. The building he constructed to house the *Lockport*

Observatory also served as the location for offices for the canal commissioners and engineers, so it truly became a prominent place in the Village of Lockport, capital of the County of Niagara.

Opportunity Beckons: A Rude Landscape Transformed

Before it actually became the county seat, Lockport had aspired to become the business and commercial center of the area, and that dream became a reality in 1822. Colonel William Bond, having developed an attachment to the village beyond its potential to make money through land sales, deeded three acres of his land to Niagara County, and the Court House/Jail and County Building were constructed on that property. A post office was established, and George H. Boughton became the first postmaster.

A rising tide of prosperity swept through the village, as many new stores and businesses were established by newcomers. John Pound migrated from Ontario County and set up the first meat market and butcher shop, In quick succession came a host of various and sundry shops, offices, and hotels: Gideon Hershey's Exchange Coffee House, William Fox's barber shop, A. T. Prentice's Jewelry Shop and Watch Repair, and the first saddle and harness shop, established by Eliot Lewis. The Eagle Hotel was built on the corner of Niagara and Prospect Streets, and the Washington House was added to a growing list of taverns and inns. Law offices multiplied. Among the most prominent lawyers were John Birdsall, Hiram Gardner, and Elias Ransom. A new road was cut through the forest from Wright's Corners to lead new settlers to Lockport, land of opportunity. A daily stagecoach ran between Lewiston and Canadaigua, another indication of Lockport's drawing power.

This surge of material activity was matched by a renewed resolution to lay the foundation for the spiritual and civic side of the community: The First Presbyterian Church was organized in 1823, along with the incorporation of the First Methodist Church. A Masonic Lodge was also chartered that same year. Its members would occupy the spotlight at the formal dedication of the locks, and assume center stage in the next decade during the infamous case of William Morgan.

The best exemplar of the spirit of enterprise was Lyman Spalding, a veritable renaissance man who founded multiple businesses and soon become a civic leader in the village and town. His was a classic Horatio Alger story, which was fortunately preserved for future historians in the form of his diaries and letters.

Spalding arrived in Lockport in 1822, traveling from Canandaigua with the intention of setting up a store, and his entrepreneurial interests multiplied thereafter. His encounter with the rude landscape that was Lockport, after hiking through the forest from the stage stop at Wrights Corners, did not prevent him from seeing the possibilities on the horizon, and he embarked upon a path that would bring him wealth and prestige in his new home town—though not without becoming enmeshed in his fair share of controversy along the way.

Almost immediately he was able to make the right connections with the leading men of the village, most of them Quakers like himself—the connections that are a defining characteristic of small towns like Lockport, from the nineteenth century through the present day. His store in Canandaigua was overstocked, so he followed a tip from Addison Comstock, son of Darius, that Lockport was the place to go. He rented a primitive building on the corner of Pine and Main Streets, observing that it was "more like a hog pen than a building," and opened up his dry goods store, stocking it with the items he brought with him from Canandaigua.

He boarded first with his friend and former employer, John C. Bond, brother of Colonel William Bond, then with Dr. Issac Smith and his wife, whose house was closer to the center of business. In 1823, he built a house on the corner of Main and Locust Streets and rented it to John Pound while boarding with the Pound Family. In 1824, he married John Pound's daughter Amy at the Friends Meeting House, and built an addition onto his original home, where he lived with his wife and their children. Things were working out very well for Lyman Spalding, as a cousin noted when he wrote him that "Lockport must be a verry money making place."

As he prospered over the next few years, he purchased land alongside the locks, and would become involved in many fields of business, from flour mills to real estate. In his peaceful pursuit of enterprise, he also gave a great deal back to his adopted community, serving in governmental offices and contributing to religious communities, above and beyond his own. His swift progress and reputation as a civic leader was made possible because he had been willing to take a chance on that burgeoning community poised on the border between the primitive setting of forest and rock, and the incipient rise of a rudimentary civilization.

Lockport was well on its way to fame. For men like Spalding and the town they were building, however, the real challenges loomed ahead. First was the job of conquering the formidable barriers presented by nature and building the locks, a mission fraught with both promise and peril. Once achieved, however, the results were astonishing. As Orsamus Turner described Lockport in the section on canal villages in his 1850 narrative history:

> This large flourishing village, now numbering its eight thousand inhabitants, its five extensive flouring mills, its Union School . . . is wholly the offspring of the Erie Canal. The site was a wilderness, dotted with but two or three log house, and stinted improvements, when the canal was located.

The transformation about to take place in Lockport was an illustration of the wisdom and confidence of Gouverneur Morris, when he had responded to the doubters in 1803. As Peter L. Bernstein recorded in *Wedding of the Waters: The Erie Canal and the Making of a Great Nation,* Simeon DeWitt viewed the prospects of building a canal with skepticism, a "romantic" notion, especially in light of the "insuperable obstacles" presented by geography. Morris responded: "*labor improbus omnia vincit*"—(the human mind devoted to improvisation could achieve anything, or roughly translated, "labor conquers all things"). Hope would spring eternal in Lockport, and in the next few years, the dream of building a canal would finally be fulfilled.

Chapter Three

ENNOBLING WORK: LOCKPORT'S MIRACLE

Lockport is, beyond comparison, the strangest looking place I ever beheld.
As far as half a dozen trees were cut down, a factory was raised up. . . . It
looks as if the demon of machinery, having invaded the peaceful realms of
nature, had fixed on Lockport as the battleground on which they should
strive for mastery. . . . The battle is lost and won, Nature is fairly routed
and driven from the field, and the rattling, crackling, hissing splitting
demon has taken possession of Lockport forever.
    —Mrs. Frances Trollope, *Domestic Manners of the Americans,* 1832

In the many books written about the Erie Canal, there is a general consensus that the canal "transformed" or "made" the nation of the United States, opening up a door to the midwest and further settlement during the nineteenth century, and the avenue to economic prosperity for the foreseeable future. And the authors—along with the contemporaries who witnessed the dream come true in 1825—recognize the fact that the most formidable obstacle to the realization of the great achievement of the Erie Canal was found at Lockport. The building of the locks there was the last task to be completed before the canal was finished.

In his introduction to *Stars in the Water,* George Condon wrote of the significance and legacy of the Erie Canal:

> It took the press of history to force the canal concept into being, to make the nation pay serious heed to its dreamers and to undertake the building of one of the longest canals in the world. Man has not ceased to marvel over the Erie Canal because it still stands out as a bold, even heroic achievement whose epic dimensions have not been diminished by time. Beyond the physical wonder of the Erie Canal, there is the political wonder that it wrought in bringing together a nation, nurturing and strengthening it until it reached full stature. . . . Its story is one of indomitable men, of wilderness, of newborn cities, of heroic immigrants, and—most of all—of a nation's pride.

When it came to writing of the famous flight of five locks, he called his chapter "The Miracle of Lockport."

Peter Bernstein's recent *Wedding of the Waters* boldly argues that "the Erie Canal was the child of many dreamers and a host of surveyors, engineers and politicians . . . the heroes of this story had the foresight to change the face of the earth." When the great gamble had succeeded against all odds, the payoff was considerable: "the end result would lead to an historic explosion of commerce, ideas, and technological change." Bernstein's discussion of what was wrought at the western end of New York is called "A Noble Work," based upon a comment made by a German tourist, Frederick Gerstaecker, who was so impressed from his vantage point at the top of the five-tiered locks that he observed that this was indeed "a noble work for so young a country."

The process of building the locks had many ripple effects in Lockport and beyond, as the visitors drawn to see the "eighth wonder of the world" recognized. Many of those visitors wrote about the speed with which the change had occurred: images like Lockport growing in "the path of a hurricane through the forest," and "the demon of machinery" engaged in a battle for the village's future and spirit. Nature had been tamed by technology as the canal progressed, and in the parlance of the time, human ingenuity and art triumphed over nature.

The Canal as America's First School of Engineering

This work of fulfillment and improvement required scientific and technological knowledge that was lacking in the new nation at the time, so ingenuity and inventiveness were called for and accompanied the progress of the canal across upstate New York. Ralph Andrist, author of *The Erie Canal,* noted that "there was no precedent in history for a canal of the Erie's length," requiring the construction of 18 aqueducts in addition to 83 locks where geography and geology made it impossible to traverse a simple, straight path.

It is often said, in fact, that the pioneering work of building the Erie Canal proved to be the first school of engineering in the young republic. After their goal was accomplished, many of the project's engineers helped found the first real school of civil engineering in the United States, the Rensselaer Polytechnic Institute (RPI) at Troy, New York in 1824.

Most of the engineers charged with building the canal had no previous training or experience in the type of work that would be required of them. According to Nobel Whitford, who wrote *History of the Canal System in New York State* in 1905, they "learned in the hard school of experience, and conquering by courage, persistence and force of character, became famous in their profession and spent lives of usefulness in their country's welfare." These men came from other walks of life, bringing their skills as surveyors and experience in the law to bear on the task ahead, learning much through the process of trial and error. More important than the material challenges of the canal project was their conviction about the larger purpose of their work and what it would mean for the future of the United States.

A small nucleus of men was largely responsible for overseeing the construction of the canal, assigned to different geographic sections as the construction proceeded from the midpoint in Rome to points east to Albany and west to Buffalo. Though the small settlement at Black Rock was also a contender for the honor of being the western terminus of the Erie Canal, Buffalo prevailed and prospered, while Black Rock ceased to exist and was absorbed by the winning city—a fine illustration of the ability of the canal to change the course of history. Of course, the work of the engineers was ultimately dependent on the thousands of Irishmen and local contractors who performed the physically difficult and dangerous labor of actually building the canal.

Benjamin Wright and James Geddes were considered the chief engineers of the entire project, ably assisted by Canvass White and John Jervis. In addition to tackling the project from the perspective of its unprecedented length, they faced the more imposing impediments of nature: rivers, valleys, forests, swamps, and mountains. No small factor in their success was the philosophical motivation that explains their sense that they were working for a higher purpose. According to Peter Bernstein, they saw nature as "less an enemy to be subdued than a gift from God to be joined in the higher struggle of building a great nation . . . as the engineers perceived it, the canal would only enhance the splendor and dignity of God's gift." The significance of this spiritual factor in helping to accomplish the tangible physicality of the grand canal would be recognized by those contemporaries who celebrated its completion with great fanfare in 1825, and by historians thereafter.

Noble Whitford offers the language of the canal commissioners in support of this perspective impressed by the fact that after the initial success at Rome, the canal craze encompassed not only the state of New York but the entire nation. In 1818 they said:

> The state of New York may indulge the proud reflection that she possesses within herself the genius, the skill, the enterprise and all the other means, requisite to the accomplishment of Internal Navigation, whose utility will surpass any work of the kind which preceding ages have accomplished. . . . What they did not understand they conquered by diligent study, unwearied zeal and common sense.

The canal commissioners and engineers were cognizant of the fact that the most difficult work was ahead of them: surviving the Montezuma Marshes (where over a thousand men died in a single season of a malaria-like illness), traversing the Genesee River at Rochester with the most imposing aqueduct on the entire canal, and the greatest challenge of all, saved for last, the escarpment at Lockport.

Triumph Over the Greatest Adversary

Assessments of the progress of the Erie Canal point out that the political obstacles that plagued Governor Clinton were secondary to the physical obstacles presented by nature. In the History Channel's *Modern Marvels* program, the narrator noted that "the idea of the canal was beautiful in its simplicity; the reality would be far more complex." It would require more than "shovels and strong backs . . . old-fashioned ingenuity and innovative tools."

Several plans were submitted, but the engineer who devised the winning proposal to overcome the escarpment at Lockport was Nathan Roberts. In an article in *The American Legion Magazine*, "How They Built the Canal," Lynwood Mark Rhodes related this anecdote about Roberts's ingenious plan, and commented that the canal commissioners had saved the "worst" for last:

> Nathan Roberts . . . cringed when he stuck a metal-tipped surveyor's rod down into the thin soil at the Niagara Escarpment. "Well, there it is," he recalled telling the Fidgety contractors. "Seven miles of limestone and flint, 30 feet thick and harder than a tax collector's heart. There is no way around it. We can't carry the water over the top. We've got to go through it."

His solution, which he considered the most triumphant achievement of his entire career, was to build a double set of five locks, for a single set was inadequate to the task of compensating for the sixty foot height differential at the Niagara escarpment.

Building the earlier sets of locks along the canal route had presented problems of their own, most notably finding a waterproof cement that was affordable. Keeping the costs of construction down was a major concern for New York's canal commissioners, especially in the face of political opposition to the "ditch" and the repeated refrain that it was a foolhardy scheme that would burden the taxpaying citizens of New York.

The engineers in training, after considering both wooden and stone locks, finally settled on stone because it would last longer. But stone locks required hydraulic cement, which was available in Europe but prohibitively expensive to import. Canvass White, the "genius of the Erie engineers" came up with the answer to this problem. Determined to find a way to manufacture the cement in the United States, he searched first in New England, and then, by chance, discovered the solution closer to the canal itself. A gray powder of pumice or lime was found near Chittenango, and it passed the waterproofing tests. This was a most important step along the way to Lockport, which, as George Condon pointed out, "would test the mettle" of the best canal workers and engineers.

Overcoming the multiple obstacles at Lockport led to several inventions, improvisations called forth by the situation and met by the ever-ready spirit of American ingenuity. Roberts's design of five double-combined locks of 12 feet each, "working side by side" in his words, was but the most spectacular of these inventions. They would become a great tourist attraction in the region throughout the nineteenth and well into the twentieth century. Because congestion on the canal was anticipated, Roberts thought it essential to create two sets of locks to handle the boats traveling both east and west, one set to help the boats descend, the other giving the illusion that boats would sail uphill as they ascended the escarpment. And the entire structure was carved through solid rock, through the use of explosives. The blasting was a defining feature of Lockport life.

Former Niagara County historian Clarence Lewis described the strenuous chores involved: "The most difficult and expensive section of the canal to be constructed was southwest of the locks, where rock excavation became necessary . . . as work progressed, the necessary rock cut became deeper and deeper, and for about three miles the average depth of the rock cut was from twenty-five to thirty feet." This "Lockport deep cut" became notoriously associated with the dangerous nature of canal work, and the accidental deaths that accompanied it.

The most noteworthy inventions brought forth by circumstances at Lockport were linked: a hardened drill able to penetrate the rock, and a newly invented blasting powder. At first, the hardened limestone proved impervious to standard drills, and many were broken in the initial attempts to create holes for the blasting powder. Appeals for adequate drills were made far and wide, to no avail. According to popular legend, a blacksmith named Botsford from nearby Niagara was finally able to solve the puzzle. He presented his invention to one of the Irish laborers, who doubted it would be able to last a minute. But he was wrong, and the new, stronger drill proved invaluable in successfully blasting the rock formation and keeping the project on schedule.

The removal of trees in the dense forest was a particularly onerous job, as was removing the rocks that had been blasted free. To handle this, devices like derricks and stump-pullers were created, often massive in size. Many pictorial representations of Lockport at the time feature regularly spaced (every 70 feet) cranes along the west bank of the canal, which lowered buckets down to the bottom of the cut for the purpose of lifting the heavy rocks up and out of the way. Credit for this invention is given to a local man named Orange Dibble. According to Historian David Dickinson of Niagara County, who contributed to the *Modern Marvels* segment, Dibble's derrick could be operated by a single horse, and was capable of lifting a ton of stone at a time. Peter Benjamin summarized the work performed at Lockport with these words:

> In the 1820s, Nathan Roberts, an engineer of limited experience, created the seven-mile Deep Cut at Lockport in three years with nothing but shovels and wheelbarrows, some animals, crude blasting powder, fragile hand-held drills, and the bare hands and broad backs of his workers. The Lockport locks were then, and remain now, the most famous structure on the Erie Canal. The achievement was all the more satisfying to those who made it possible, given the odds against its success; in sum, it was nothing less than a man-made miracle.

Acute Growing Pains of a Boom Town

The village of Lockport was thoroughly transformed by the work performed there in those three short years, and the ripple effects of the changes would reverberate throughout the community for decades. Initially, most of the attention of the settlers and visitors alike was focused on the physical changes. But those changes led to social and cultural changes that were equally far-reaching.

Although there were no ceremonies to mark the turning of the first shovel of earth for the canal construction at Lockport, the *Lockport Observatory* newspaper took note of the local activity and progress in October of 1822: "The excavation of the canal through the Mountain Ridge at this place is progressing in a manner highly advantageous to the state and creditable to the contractors. There are now employed on the canal, in and near this village, about eleven hundred men; and the amount of money daily expended by the contractors is rising of $1,000." This sentiment of pride and hopeful expectation for the future, though premature, was understandable.

The phenomenal growth, however, was not without its problems. According to tradition, the Erie Canal was built by Irish immigrants. Local workers were also regularly employed, but there was a real infusion of immigrant laborers into Lockport in 1821, many responding to the advertisements placed by Nathan Roberts in New York City newspapers. This Irish flavor left its permanent mark on the town and city. Ronald Shaw, in his 1966 history of the Erie Canal, *Erie Water West,* offered a succinct summary of the effects of the arrival of Irish canal workers:

> All was bustle and vigor as Lockport sprouted to become a village. . . . But here, too, rapid growth was accompanied by acute growing pains. Newcomers scrambled for lots, shortages drove prices high, and the Irish laborers engaged in lusty combat over Old County loyalties.

More insight into these "acute growing pains" can be gained from an examination of nineteenth century accounts. In "Recollections of an Old Settler," Ednah Smith devotes a considerable amount of attention to the place of the Irish in her community. The "army of Irish" laborers were usually housed in shanties or crude communities on the outskirts of town, keeping them remote from the center of civilized life in the village. Several of these are mentioned in accounts written during the 1820s: Cottonburg, Lanesburg near Pendleton, and even an "Irish row" or Irish Road. Aunt Ednah, like most of her contemporaries, was ambivalent toward the presence of so many "wild" Irish in the community, tolerating them as a "necessary evil." Though they were needed to toil on the canal, it was generally hoped that once their dirty and dangerous work was completed they would move on, perhaps heading west to dig the canals in Ohio, Michigan, and beyond. Many of the more established settlers, while acknowledging their moral obligation to "uplift" those below them in status or class, also expressed a genuine dread of the unruly lot of Irishmen in their midst. George Condon described the nature of this feeling in Lockport:

> Though their handiwork alone gave Lockport its reason for existence, the Irish canal builders were not popular members of the growing community; even to describe them as members of the community might be stretching words. Segregation was the order of the day. . . . The townspeople made it a point to avoid unnecessary association with the crude, strange-sounding foreigners, not necessarily from a sense of snobbery. Fear, decidedly, was an element that shaped the attitudes of the community.

Mrs. Smith recounted several episodes of conflict in Lockport, Taking note of the "bitter feeling between the Orangemen and the Catholics" she acknowledged the presence of a sea of religious as well as ethnic divisions that would be re-visited in the community's formative years. Recalling processions of armed men in honor of the Battle of the Boyne and St. Patrick's Day, she commented that "the whole state of feeling on those days was such that it needed but a word or breath to set battle and bloodshed going." She also referred to the "Irish element" and the "hot blood of that nation:"

> Away from the restraints of a settled town, it needed all the force and vigilance at command to prevent wild work now and then. . . . Mobs and riots occurred occasionally, originating generally from quarrels among themselves . . . but they usually ended in nothing more serious than a few broken heads and black eyes, or once in a while a shanty town torn down or dismantled, but the inhabitants were always alarmed at such times, not knowing when the spirit of mischief would end, once loosed from restraints.

Clearly, the "proper citizens" of Lockport were wary of the effect of the Irish invasion upon their community. Having begun the work of civilizing the wilderness that was early Lockport, the Irish now posed a threat to the sense of law and order that was in the process of formation.

Aunt Ednah added to her sense of alarm by making some observations of the way they lived on a daily basis: "men, Protestant and Catholic, slept promiscuously" and became enraged over political discussions, which often commenced in "free fights." Although the "array of black and bruised bodies was fearful to behold," to their credit, "there was seldom any ill blood or revengeful feelings left after the battle was once ended." An element of ambivalence was also present in these recollections: Mrs. Smith could be moved to compassion. Testifying to the dangers of the blasting and falling rocks, she remembered "many a poor fellow who was blown to fragments . . . on some days, the list of killed and wounded would be almost like those of a battlefield."

As the wife of a physician who was sometimes called to give emergency medical treatment to the Irish, she was also witness to cases of suffering and touching episodes of love that illustrated the potentially devastating effects of ethnic and religious prejudice. A very refined Englishwoman, married to an Irishman of whom her family disapproved, was forced to give birth to her first child in "a wretched shanty, about as forlorn a condition as one would well imagine. The couple, emigrating from Canada, had been reduced to the condition of common Irish laborers." But the husband, "noble, intelligent and fine-looking," eventually triumphed over adversity by working as a bookkeeper, moving to Rochester, and eventually becoming mayor of that city—"and they lived happily ever after."

Violence Unleashed—Strikes and Riots

Despite the mixed emotions expressed by Aunt Ednah Smith and other citizens of Lockport, their fears that the Irish presented a real threat to order and safety were eventually realized. On at least two documented occasions, armed conflicts or "riots" occurred, symptoms of the exploitation and alienation experienced by the Irish workers who were often regarded as little better than slave labor by many contractors.

In his 1993 monograph *Common Labor: Workers and the Digging of North American Canals, 1780–1860*, British Historian Peter Way focused on the canal workers and the culture they created. Way's labor history has a bit of a Marxist slant to it, as he argues that the "canallers" were often "agents of change." This was certainly true in Lockport, which merits analysis in the book—a part of Lockport's history that has often been overlooked. The Irish immigrants were subject to simmering pressures that periodically erupted in violence in many spots along the canal routes. Their exploits in Lockport had significant consequences in the public arena and serve as the most graphic examples of civil unrest and strife in the rapidly growing community.

Several local chroniclers have mentioned the Lockport riots of 1822 and 1824, at the height of the canal construction. Niagara County historian Clarence Lewis, who made such a valuable contribution by preserving the story of Lockport's past, wrote in a series of articles on "Lockport and the Erie Canal" that "the log cabin village was the scene of frequent riots and strikes among the Irish laborers, with an occasional necessity of calling upon the militia to restore order. Two or three were killed . . . many were injured by flying stones. Whiskey was almost as plentiful as water . . . contractors bought it for $4.50 a barrel and dispensed it freely to the workmen, believing it resulted in more work by the men." This combustible mix of liquor and class/ethnic tension spilled over on two famous occasions, when violence erupted for a variety of reasons.

The first occurred in 1822, and became known as the Christmas Eve Riot. Several local newspapers of the day carried stories about it, containing many stereotypes about the Irish. By all accounts, it was a case of the wild and unruly laborers suffering the effects of overindulging in whiskey, or "getting fairly in their cups." A crowd, estimated at 40 or 50 men, gathered in front of the J. P. Lawes Tavern on Canal Street and soon turned into a mob. The exact cause of the "provocation" was unknown. Bent upon the destruction of the tavern, however, the Irish commenced hurling rocks through the windows. According to the *Rochester Telegraph* story, "the scene soon changed from a pitched battle to a riot, which excited considerable uneasiness among the citizens . . . stones flew as thick as blackberries, and bludgeons were brandishing in every direction. Two persons were mortally wounded."

Twelve Irishmen were arrested and imprisoned—in the jails of neighboring communities, as Lockport's jail and courthouse building was not yet completed—and 20 were said to have escaped to Canada.

The main casualty of the conflict was John Jennings, and several people were subsequently indicted for his murder. The Lewiston paper in October of 1823 reported that "the Special Court of Oyer and Terminer, appointed for the trial of persons implicated in the riot at Lockport on Christmas Eve last, commenced its session on Tuesday, Judge William B. Rochester presiding."

This was the first trial ever held at Lockport, and to guard against any interruption, villagers maintained an armed guard around the Mansion House where the trial was held. The trial occasioned by the "unhappy riot," according to the Lewiston *Sentinel,* was the scene of "arguments of some of the ablest lawyers in this State, on the several points of riot, murder, manslaughter and justifiable homicide." Although the main defendant, James Kelley, was found innocent of murder, he was convicted of manslaughter. He and several other men were sentenced to prison terms for their part in the riot.

Minor disturbances were not uncommon, and Historian Lewis observed that "villagers, especially women, were under a constant tension." One such incident was recalled by one of the women, a Mrs. Bailey Whitcher. Because her husband was out of town, she was spending the night with her friend Mrs. Joel Hall. The timid young women were afraid of staying alone, given the recurrent violence, and barricaded themselves in the house. Awakened about 10:00 p.m. by men quarreling outside the house, they heard shrieks and groans, and the sounds of rocks flying. Fearful of staying in the house, they climbed out a rear window and ran to George LeValley's house. LeValley had a kiln, and prepared a kettle of hot lye to be used to defend the women, if it became necessary. But there was no further trouble, and they remained at LeValley's overnight. The next morning, when they returned to Mrs. Hall's house, they found the snow surrounding the house stained with blood—the fatal feud was attributed to whiskey. The women of the community decided to start a temperance movement as a result of this incident and others like it, and Lockport became known as a center of the temperance movement during the antebellum reform era.

The second major riot occurred in July of 1824, and was noteworthy as the first instance in U.S. history of the state militia being called out to quell a labor disturbance. It was a conflict sparked by religious tensions—Protestant vs. Catholic—within the Irish community. The Lewiston newspaper devoted a lengthy piece to the "Battle of the Kegs," noting that it was an "unharmonious occurrence." On July 12, 1824—the anniversary of the landing of King William in Ireland—"many of the Orange Loyalists laboring on the 'great ditch' in the vicinity of Lockport had planned a celebration." The patronizing tone of the piece underscores the sentiments felt by many of the Yankees toward the Irish—especially the Catholic Irish—in their community:

> On this, as on all like occasions in the land of Potatoes, the indignation of the votaries of St. Patrick was aroused. *When Pat meets Pat, then comes the tug of war.* Shelalies, brick-bats and stone missiles were in high requisition; and as numerical force is wont to prevail, the friends of King William were constrained to yield the palm to their Catholic superiors. This state of things, which held the sober Yankees of Lockport in terrorem, was not to be tolerated with impunity.
>
> Luckily, it chanced to be a day of militia drilling, and a gallant corps of republican riflemen were then exercising within nine miles of the scene of turmoil. . . . The brave riflemen, with the patriotic volunteers of Lockport . . . on arriving at the expected scene of commotion, to their inexpressible disappointment, found nothing but the snorings of Bacchus where they had anticipated the groans of the dying. The happy termination of the expedition, we are told, is mainly attributable to the good conduct and prudence of the sheriff . . . who ordered the music to apprise them of their danger. . . . We are happy to learn that the campaign was brought to a close without the loss of a single life, though much whiskey was shed and many a nose waxed red before the veterans could be persuaded to retire to the shades of peacefulness.

As reported in the *Rochester Telegraph*, the story was much the same: differing religious and political opinions among the Irish, split into camps of Orangemen and Catholics, spilled over into armed conflict. The Catholics were charged with "threatening to put to death every Orangeman," and were portrayed as the chief source of trouble. This report, however, noted that the mob had been awed into submission by the militia, and that they "must have convinced the rioters that the means are at hand at all times to punish their outrages. . . . No lives were lost . . . and the laborers have assumed their usual peaceable appearance."

The message of the public authority, and the lesson learned by the community, was perfectly clear—the threat to law and order posed by the wild Irish, even when it was exaggerated, was a painful reality in the canal town. The Irish were beyond the pale of the civilized society, and could be intimidated into submission if they threatened the peace. Though it was acknowledged that the Irish laborers generally worked hard and well at the dangerous tasks required of them as occupants at the bottom of the ethnic, religious, and socio-economic ladder, vigilance on the part of their "superiors" was necessary. The story of the building of the canal, it seems, was one of the "breaking down of an old world as much as the building of the new." Way's analysis, when applied to Lockport, alternated themes of fragmentation and integration as "confusion and conflict emerged" along the way toward the building of a community consensus.

But consensus would not prevail in Lockport for some time. Businesses continued to grow, and with the arrival of new settlers, churches and community organizations multiplied. The most noteworthy fraternal organization, in terms of Lockport's future, was the local chapter of the Freemasons. In 1824, the Ames Royal Arch Chapter 88 was chartered, and the Lockport Lodge was formed at the Niagara Hotel. The Masons would soon be mired in controversy, as the nation's attention was riveted on Lockport and its surroundings during the trial that followed the mysterious disappearance of a former Mason planning to expose the secrets of the organization.

For the immediate future however, the community's attention was focused on finishing the work of the locks and on the upcoming formal ceremonies to mark the opening of the canal in 1825. Lockport was a microcosm of the changes that had occurred across upstate New York since De Witt Clinton first proposed his impossible dream, when the general reaction to the idea was skepticism at best and lunacy at worst. In *Wedding of the Waters,* Bernstein stated that one of Clinton's political enemies made reference to the enterprise in these terms: "to construct a railroad from the earth to the moon could not be treated with more derision."

Nevertheless, by 1824 the end goal was in sight, the dream about to be fulfilled—and Lockport would have a starring role in the great national drama of creating a new era in American history.

Chapter Four

DE WITT CLINTON'S
MISSION ACCOMPLISHED

AT LOCKPORT—the spot where the waters were to meet when the last blow was struck, and where the utility of an immense chain of locks was for the first time to be tested, the Celebration was in all respects such as to do honor to the work itself, and the patriotic feelings of the people. It is here that nature has interposed her strongest barrier to the enterprise and strength of man. But the massive granite of the "Mountain Ridge" was compelled to yield. The rocks have crumbled to pieces and been swept away, and the waters of Erie flow tranquilly in their place.
   —William L. Stone, *Narrative of the Festivities Observed in Honor of the Completion of the Grand Erie Canal Uniting the Waters of the Great Western Lakes with the Atlantic Ocean*, 1825

The year 1825 proved to be a historic one for New York state and the nation, for it marked the completion of the Grand Erie Canal, the fulfillment of Governor DeWitt Clinton's vision. This mission was accomplished after years of unrelenting work, from the time when a young politician first hitched his wagon—or, more appropriately, his barge—to the star of canal navigation. The occasion was one of grand celebration. William Stone's commemorative account noted that it was "begun in Buffalo, on the twenty-sixth of October, A.D., Eighteen Hundred and Twenty-Five, and ended in the City of New York, on the Fourth Day of November." The extravagance and duration of the festivities was something unparalleled in the young republic's history, and one that was not soon superseded. The overall tenor of the celebration was of triumph and faith in the notion that the American nation was now destined for great things, with the state of New York rising to become the Empire State. Those who organized and participated in the events that took place along the entire route of the canal had a deep and abiding sense of history, confident that these days would long be remembered by posterity.

As for Lockport's place in this great spectacle, its course now seemed determined. It was the location of the greatest engineering feature of the entire canal, and much attention was focused on the small village in the days leading up to, during, and after the celebration that culminated in the symbolic Wedding of the Waters. But now that it had arrived at the moment of its finest hour in the national spotlight, Lockport's grand adventure was just beginning. It would prove to be a very auspicious year.

De Witt Clinton's Fame and New York's Fortune

As always, Lockport's story can only be understood against the backdrop of the canal. As progress continued, so too did the fortunes of the town. The path was not without its setbacks, but Clinton stayed focused on the goal and was ultimately vindicated. He possessed a genuine talent for articulating the greater purpose every step of the way.

Yet his political foes continued to try to thwart him. In 1824, they struck a cruel blow and removed him from the office of canal commissioner. According to Clinton's first biographer, David Hosack, this move backfired and he was re-elected governor in 1825: "It produced an almost universal re-action in his favour . . . he calmly retired until the storm then raging might be expended, when he again rose superior to his enemies, and in every misfortune with which they had endeavored to overwhelm him." Time and time again, De Witt Clinton persevered in the face of whatever adversity came his way, and he emerged victorious at the end. As governor of New York, he would preside over the ceremonies marking the fulfillment of his dream.

There was a certain poignancy in the fact that after living to see his ambitions achieved, he died in 1828 at the height of his fame. The New York Literary and Philosophical Society, "deeply sensible of their loss"—for Clinton had served as the Society's president as well as governor—resolved to pronounce a "discourse commemorative of the worth and services of the deceased." Dr. David Hosack was charged with the task of writing that discourse, and the resulting *Memoir of De Witt Clinton* provides a good record of Clinton's life and its guiding light, the Erie Canal.

Written as a hagiography of the man whose fame had become identified with the "origin, progress and completion of the Canals of this state," Hosack's memoir is filled with the imagery and language of the early nineteenth century. It served as an expression of the bereavement of the inhabitants of New York City, "which, by his genius, virtues and untiring exertions, has been rendered the seat of commerce, prosperity and opulence:"

> His energy and influence and foresight intermingled the Lakes and the Hudson. The great Western Canal owns him as its efficient patron. . . . He viewed, in its completion, the prosperity of the state and the glory of the nation. And on its accomplishment he hazarded his renown. The pledge was nobly given. That work alone will immortalize his name, and the benefits resulting from it will transcend the power of computation.

Dr. Hosack put Clinton in the company of the great men of world history, for "he exhibited in his conduct the example of a stern and inflexible republican, in the large and catholic sense of the term, worthy of the purest period of Grecian or Roman History, and to which, at this day, parallels can be found on no spot of the habitable globe, but in our own county."

Placing both De Witt Clinton and the American nation in such august company was in keeping with the prevailing spirit at the ceremonies marking the completion of the canal three years before the governor's passing.

Hosack called him "the popular divinity" at the canal celebration in Albany in 1823, and noted that an eminent counselor of the New York bar saw Clinton as "the Pericles of our commonwealth." Hosack also declared that Clinton, thanks to his "gigantic" and "stupendous" achievement, deserved to be elevated and assigned a place, as a matter of justice, with "those of Washington, Hamilton, Franklin, Adams, Rittenhouse, Jefferson, Fulton and other American worthies." He would be admired for keeping the cause of the canal alive, and "will ever be identified with the existence of his country, and transmitted with increasing luster to the latest posterity." Hyperbole notwithstanding, Hosack's assessment was an accurate one, and he was correct in making the first real claim that "the existence of the New York canal will ever be identified with the name and fame of De Witt Clinton." In terms of the site of the famous locks on the Niagara escarpment, Clinton would also be remembered for having the prescience to see the area's potential before the village of Lockport was born.

Preparing for the Opening of the Canal by Welcoming Lafayette

Prior to the state-wide celebration to commemorate the official opening of the canal in 1825, Lockport was the scene of two noteworthy events: the visit of General Lafayette to the village as part of his tour of the United States, and the official laying of the capstone at the base of the locks on June 24. But regular development in the village continued in the months leading up that occasion, as the town continued to grow. Among the less spectacular events recorded in Lockport history were the appointment of Asa Douglass as the first toll collector, and the election of Eli Bruce as sheriff. The first proper fire company in Lockport was organized, and the courthouse and jail building was finally completed. A decision by the New York legislature would have a significant effect on Lockport, and would be the source of much controversy over the next several years. A law authorizing the sale of water rights from the canal was passed, and it was quickly recognized that this water could be harnessed for the power to run businesses. The town and some of its leading citizens, including Lyman Spalding, would be preoccupied with determining who owned the rights to the water that would one day lead to the village becoming the city of smokeless power.

But in June of 1825, all attention shifted to preparing for the visit of the great French general and hero of the American Revolution, the Marquis de Lafayette. In the last year of his administration President James Monroe had prevailed upon Congress to extend an invitation to his old friend to visit the United States one last time. This triumphal tour took Lafayette to every state in the nation, so that he could assess and see how successful the American experiment had become since the days of the Revolution. The Erie Canal proved to be, quite naturally, a major attraction, and the towns in upstate New York were anxious to host the "Nation's Guest" with much fanfare. Lockport was no exception.

As Lafayette made his way along the route, he was amazed at what had been accomplished and recorded his impressions of the canal and the warm welcome he received everywhere he went. As he paid his respects to the canal his secretary

Levasseur, who kept the journal of the trip, applauded the feats of the engineers: "the bridges are usually of an elegance and boldness of execution that is inconceivable." The general marveled at the aqueducts and observed that the canal appeared to "pursue an aerial route" at the location of those impressive structures, sometimes "for more than a quarter of a mile, at an elevation of 70 feet." The famous set of five locks, even more impressive, would elicit more grandiose comments.

Arriving at Buffalo on a Lake Erie steamboat, Lafayette made his way to the Eagle Tavern, where he was greeted by the now customary celebration. The next day, he was determined to view the cataract at Niagara Falls, and visited Fort Niagara where military honors awaited him. In a special 1965 commemorative edition of the Lockport *Union-Sun & Journal,* issued on the 100th anniversary of the incorporation of the city, an article entitled "Enthusiastic Welcome Received in Lockport by Gen. Lafayette" appeared. Covering his tour of the entire Niagara region, it was noted that he was "so impressed by Goat Island that he lingered there for a long time and was tempted to buy it when Judge Porter offered to sell it!" Moving on to Lewiston, he passed by the Tuscarora Indian Reservation, where he encountered a Chief Cusick. This tribal leader had once fought with the general, and was "affectionately greeted" by his old friend.

As the Lafayette company made its way to Lockport on June 6, he was greeted at numerous taverns. At Howell's Creek he enjoyed a refreshing lemonade (an experience recalled years later by the young Howell Daughter), and was greeted at John Gould's Tavern on the Lower Mountain Road by an advance Lockport team showing him the requisite respect and hospitality even before he arrived in the village. The route to Lockport from this point onward was through a dense forest, and the group emerged at Prospect Street. Determined to impress General Lafayette in singular fashion, elaborate preparations had been made to welcome him.

Canal workers had planted gunpowder charges in the rock wall, and lit the fuses to produce a hundred "gun" salute, because there were no cannon available. Lafayette was so taken with this show, which he thought was artillery, that he exclaimed, "the very rocks rend to welcome me." A delegation of citizens then escorted him to the Washington House for a gala celebration. Here he was introduced by Stephen Van Rensselaer of the Canal Commission, and Lockport local Daniel Washburn served as the toastmaster at the dinner. Lafayette responded with a most memorable toast of his own, which has been proudly recorded in every local history of the city since that day: "To Lockport and the County of Niagara, containing the greatest natural and artificial wonders second only to the wonders of Freedom and Equal Rights." With these words, Lockport's place in the grand American pageant of republican values, scientific ingenuity, and business enterprise was assured.

Next Lafayette, his son George Washington Lafayette, and his secretary were escorted to the Masonic Hall on the banks of the canal—a prelude to the upcoming festivities later that year, where the Masons would be prominently featured. Finally, he was escorted to the locks, still under construction but well on the way to completion. A band began to play, and the entourage boarded a festively decorated packet boat for the trip to Rochester. According to Historian Clarence Lewis, another round of blasts was set off, "giving the General a most thrilling farewell." All of the time and effort to provide another "blaze of glory" was not in vain, for Lafayette spoke of the locks forever after as "that stupendous piece of engineering work in Lockport"—a sentiment with which many subsequent visitors, humble and esteemed alike, would agree. In summing up the effects of this historic trip, the general's secretary wrote at length of his lasting impressions of the place carved out of the wilderness:

> I have nowhere seen the activity and industry of man brought into operation against natural difficulties as in this young village . . . the sound of axe and hammer are everywhere heard . . . the falling trees made into houses . . . and a schoolhouse and a press . . . and finally, in the midst of these encroachments of civilization on savage nature, that great canal is proceeding with a rapidity which seems to mark the hand of union . . . and will, at the same time, diffuse life and abundance in the deserts though which it passes.

Laying of the Capstone at the Locks

Later that month, on June 24, the village celebrated the next event in the momentous year of 1825—a most joyous and solemn occasion arising solely from Lockport. It was this particular ceremony that was most evocative of the swirling ideological tides prevalent in the United States during the "Era of Good Feelings:" republican virtue, rising democratic values, and the expectation of unprecedented prosperity and progress on the horizon. As Carol Sheriff explained in *The Artificial River*, these American sentiments were also colored with mixed feelings about the triumph of "art" over nature, and what changes would follow in the wake of the successfully completed canal. For the triumph of art, it was hoped, meant both the physical and the moral progress of society. This philosophy was best expressed in the words carved on the capstone:

ERIE CANAL
Let posterity be excited to perpetuate our
Free Institutions.
And to make still greater efforts than their ancestors to promote
Public Prosperity:
By the recollection that these works of Internal Improvement
Were achieved by the
Spirit and Perseverance of
Republican Freemen

The stone also noted that "The Erie Canal, 362 miles in length, was commenced on the 4th of July 1817, And completed in the year 1825 at an expense of about $7,000,000 and was constructed exclusively By the Citizens of the State of NEW YORK." A small brass plate with the following subdued inscription also marks the beginning of what was accomplished at Lockport: "The first stone of these locks was laid on the 9th of July, 1823, by N. S. Roberts, engineer, and Samuel Horn, master workman, in the presence of citizens of this place."

The centerpiece of the ceremony accompanying the laying of the capstone of the Ten Combined Locks at Lockport was an address delivered by the Reverend F. H. Cuming, Rector of St. Luke's Episcopalian Church, Rochester, to an audience of four to five thousand, gathered around the locks. In the printed version of the address, as requested by the Ames Chapter of Royal Arch Masons when they gave the job to Orsamus Turner, it is noted on the cover that June 24 was "the anniversary of St. John the Baptist," considered a patron of the Masonic Order. The Masons would be prominent actors on the Lockport stage in the early nineteenth century, a small-town illustration of the prevalence and influence of the order in early American history. Many of the founding fathers and leading politicians of the young republic were Masons, including George Washington, Benjamin Franklin, and Chief Justice John Marshall. When Lafayette visited, the fact that he was a Mason was well known, acknowledged, and honored in the festivities surrounding his visit. Dr. David Hosack, in singing the praises of De Witt Clinton in his *Memoir*, took note of this Masonic connection and influence and went on to recognize that many "illustrious" politicians, as well as "dignitaries of the church and clergy of different denominations" belonged to the order, which was the "most unequivocal evidence of the purity of the principles, the correct morals, and the religious tendency of the precepts masonry inculcates." But he also acknowledged some of the opposition to and controversy surrounding Masonry at the time, when he wrote of the "unworthy" as well as "meritorious" members typical of other benevolent institutions, just as "Christianity has its Pharisees as well as its sincere worshippers." But he concludes his assessment of the Masonic order and its famous members on a positive note, saying it had received the "uniform support" of the best of men, "distinguished for their intelligence, integrity and piety."

The Reverend Cuming was certainly perceived as one of those "best of men," a Mason as well as a Christian minister, who was deemed worthy of the honor of speaking on this historic occasion. In the course of his address, he repeatedly pointed out the links between the building of the canal and the work of the founding fathers in creating the United States, and the fact that leaders in both endeavors were members of the Masonic fraternity. Another pervasive theme was the fact that what had been accomplished in Lockport was unprecedented and truly remarkable—the stuff of future legends.

Cuming began by summoning the spirits of the dead who would have welcomed the achievement as a fitting addendum to the cause of liberty – Edmund Burke and "our beloved Washington." His extravagant style of speaking, stretching the imagination to best appreciate the wonders of the undertaking, characterized the entire address and was no doubt pleasing to his audience.

He referred to Lockport as a "romantic place," which was a vast wilderness just four years before but had risen to become "a most interesting village, with 1,500 inhabitants, a noble hall of justice, extensive ware-houses, numerous workshops and well-filled stores."

Taking note of the practical effects of the canal, Cuming spoke of how this work had given an opportunity to many "when they could find employment nowhere else," and predicted that "public revenue would be much increased" and that it was "only in New York that there exists this noble system of internal improvements." Only at Lockport could one behold such a "splendid specimen of Masonic Architecture; most striking and finished point on the whole line of New York's Grand Canal." Even though there was a mile of excavating work still to be done, he considered the "mighty work as now finished" and added that it was fitting to exclaim: "The mountains have been leveled, the vallies have been filled . . . by the exertions of art."

The most resounding portion of this paean to the canal and the locks came at the end, just as Cuming was admonished for speaking too long and getting carried away with his assignment; nevertheless, his rhetorical flourish was unrestrained:

> The work is done. The long labor is over. Let us bless God, the Supreme Architect, that we have lived to see it accomplished. Let us bless God, that we lived in the year which will forever be so proudly distinguished in our country's history.

Reverend Cuming's tendency to invoke the almighty would be echoed in three months when the state of New York, with the eyes of the nation focused on it, staged the most extravagant celebration of all—a fantastic event that would culminate in the Wedding of the Waters.

Wedding of the Waters—Clinton's Faith Sustained

The climax of the 10 day extravaganza that marked the completion of the Erie Canal was the moment when Governor De Witt Clinton dramatically poured a keg of Lake Erie water into the Atlantic, symbolizing the connection between the ocean and the Great Lakes. As Peter Bernstein wrote of that day, the governor's task also memorialized "all the years of hope and anger, progress and retreat, and design and redesign that led up to this moment." As he performed this ceremony of mingling the waters, Clinton waxed eloquent about the significance of what New York had achieved:

> The solemnity, at this place, on the first arrival of vessels from Lake Erie is intended to indicate and commemorate the navigable communication, which has been accomplished between our Mediterranean Seas and the Atlantic ocean, in about eight years, to the extent of more than four hundred and twenty-five miles, by the wisdom, public spirit, and the energy of the people of the state of New York.

Leading up to this long-awaited hour on November 4, 1825 was the parade of boats that started in Buffalo and traversed the entire length of the canal and the Hudson River, stopping at numerous towns along the way including Lockport. The entire affair was a spectacular production from beginning to end, including a ball in New

York City on the night of November 7. In *The Wedding of the Waters*, Peter Bernstein contends that "the most lavish impresarios of our own time . . . never staged anything as elaborate or prolonged," and that "the most impressive feature of the whole series of events was the stamina of the participants."

The "Festivities Observed in Honor of the Completion of the Grand Erie Canal" commenced in Buffalo on the morning of October 26. Cadwallader D. Colden, grandson of the man who had been one of the first to envision the construction of an artificial river back in the eighteenth century upon a visit to the Mohawk Valley, preserved a detailed record of the combined events in his Memoir, with William L. Stone contributing another lengthy narrative at the request of the Committee of the Corporation of the City of New York. According to George Condon, "The formal opening of the Erie Canal was made memorable by many things, but none more than the devastating torrent of words which it unloosed throughout the state. Speechmakers . . . pulled out all the oratorical stops in praise of the great waterway." A tone of hyperbole, symbolism, and unfettered pride captured the spirit of the event.

The main focus of the celebration was the flotilla of ships that would be the first to travel on the canal from beginning to end. First was the *Seneca Chief*, which carried the man of the year and his party, including Lieutenant Governor Tallmadge. No expense was spared in the outfitting of this packet boat. It contained wooden kegs decorated with gilded hoops and eagles, and the cabin was adorned with a grand painting that depicted Clinton, regaled in a Roman costume and having just opened the lock gate and invited Neptune, god of the sea, to join him, while Hercules, renowned for completing impossible tasks, rests. Next in the procession of boats were the *Superior*, *Commodore Perry*, and *Buffalo.* The most interesting in the long line that followed was the *Noah's Ark*. As the name implied, its cargo consisted of assorted birds and beasts from the west, and two Native American boys in their traditional dress.

The honor of delivering the first address, before the boats were boarded at Buffalo, was rightfully reserved for Jesse Hawley, whose Hercules essays two decades before first made the vision of a canal seem realistic. Hawley spoke of the canal on this occasion as "a work that will constitute the lever of industry, population and wealth to our Republic—a pattern for our Sister States to imitate—an exhibition of the moral force of a free and enlightened people to the world." He also paid tribute to "the projectors who devised, the statesmen who assumed the responsibility of the undertaking . . . the legislators who granted the supplies, the commissioners who planned, the engineers who laid out, and the men who executed this magnificent work."

At the conclusion of Hawley's speech, a cannon signaled the start of an artillery salute and relay, designed to convey news of the celebration and the progress of the flotilla so that the many events planned along the route could be properly timed. At regular intervals along the route from Buffalo to Sandy Hook, New Jersey on New York harbor, the guns steadily fired. Then, the cannonade was reversed. The entire process took over two hours, and the boats left for Lockport. Colden, recalling the moment when he heard the cannon, wrote: "Who that has American blood in his veins can hear this sound without emotion? Who that has the privilege to do it, can refrain from exclaiming, I too am an American citizen; and feel as much pride in being able to make that declaration, as ever an inhabitant of the eternal city felt, in proclaiming that he was a Roman." Clearly, the men who participated in these festivities expected that these days would be long remembered on a par with the achievements of ancient civilizations.

The floating parade was next joined by the *Niagara* from Black Rock, with Peter Porter on board. Though he had lost out to Buffalo in his quest to have Black Rock named the western terminus of the canal, any lingering feelings of resentment were apparently assuaged by the fact that the canal was now a reality. The next stop was Lockport, where, according to Condon's history, "the welcoming ceremony was especially elaborate." From the visit of LaFayette through the laying of the capstone, Lockport had been in an almost continuous state of festivity—with much pomp and circumstance held in reserve for this day.

Contemporary accounts devote a good deal of attention to Lockport's place in the celebration, and its paramount importance in the history of the canal. Colden notes:

> The deep cutting towards the western extremity of this section has cost more money, and required more labor, than any other work on the Canals. To pass the mountain ridge, there has been a necessity for excavating seven miles . . . three miles of which is through hard rock. The combined locks, at the brow of the mountain, the commissioners describe as a work of the first magnitude on the line, and as one of the greatest of its kind in the world.

William Stone's narrative pauses at Lockport, reporting that "on the morning of the twenty-sixth, a salute was fired from the mountain adjoining the locks, and ere long the place was crowded . . . many individuals . . . from distant parts of the state, and from other states, attended the celebration at this interesting place." Several of the distinguished guests formed a procession, and embarked on the packet-boat *William C. Bouck*, named for one of the canal commissioners, as the rest of the flotilla was joined to ascend the mountain ridge:

> This Basin, connected with the stupendous succession of locks . . . is one of the most interesting places on the route, if not in the world, and presents one of the most striking evidences of human power and enterprise which has hitherto been witnessed. A double set of locks, whose workmanship will vie with the most splendid monuments of antiquity, rise majestically, one after the other, to the height of sixty-three feet: the surplus water is conducted around them, and furnishes some of the finest mill-seats imaginable. A marble tablet modestly tells the story of their origin: and without that vanity, which, though frequently laudable, is often carried to excess, imputes their existence to our Republican institutions.

This occasion marked the first time the locks had ever been used, and the event was recognized by the firing of a 32 pound cannon as a band began to play. It was a special cannon, once used on a ship in Commodore Oliver Hazard Perry's fleet during the War of 1812, in the Battle of Lake Erie, and it was fired by a Frenchman who had once fought with Napoleon. Thousands of rock blasts prepared for the occasion, like those used to welcome LaFayette in June, followed. In a lengthy story published in the *Lockport Observatory* on October 29, 1825, more details of the day's events were provided—with all the local pride the newspaper could muster, for it was the "duty" of the publisher to give such a sketch. The 26th day of October, according to the *Observatory*, "will be remembered and celebrated as the auspicious period when the mighty labors of a great, persevering and patriotic people were crowned with abundant success."

The boats then moved westward to meet the fleet approaching from Buffalo. Once arrived, Governor Clinton joined the assembled celebrities, including Enos Boughton of Lockport, "venerable pioneer of the Western district who had planted the first orchard west of Utica," at a "well-prepared table" at the Washington House. D. Washburn, Esq., presided over the evening's activities, which consisted of multiple toasts abounding in superlatives and claims of greatness. Throughout the evening the village was brilliantly illuminated, in keeping with the wish that this night would never end.

One touching aside was also printed in this edition of the *Observatory*—an exception to the general rule of the day, which focused on the rich and famous members of society while neglecting the poor workers. Titled "Unfortunate Occurrence," it was reported: "drowned in this village, this morning, Orrin Harrison, one of the workingmen employed at the locks . . . from excessive fatigue fell asleep" and was "precipitated" into eight feet of water in one of the locks. "His legs dragged through the gates," and, "before he could be extricated, life became extinct." A marker was later erected at the site to note his passing.

The rest of the celebration continued along the route of the canal, with several noteworthy episodes worth mentioning. At Rochester, the *Young Lion of the West* joined the parade, and cried out to the lead boat: "Who comes there?" followed by the response "Your brothers from the West, on the waters of the great lakes." At the town of Rome, whose fortunes had suffered when the final canal route passed it by, the locals carried a black barrel filled with water from the old canal and dumped it into the new canal; however, once their protest was registered they joined the upbeat mood of the day, honoring the completion of the canal.

At New York City, following Clinton's formal performance of the wedding of the waters, excess abounded when a friend of the governor went on to empty 13 bottles of water—from rivers such as the Ganges, Amazon, Nile, Rhine, and the Mississippi— into the Atlantic Ocean, marking the world-wide significance of the occasion. Colden and Stone's commemorative pieces also report on a concluding parade or grand procession on Manhattan Island, accompanied by chants from an ode composed by Samuel Woodworth:

> 'Tis done! 'Tis done! The mighty chain
> Which joins bright Erie to the Main,
> For ages shall perpetuate
> The glory of our native state!

George Condon called the entire affair "the most wonderful demonstration by far that New York ever had seen—indeed, that any American city ever had seen." In "Rational Exultation: the Erie Canal Celebration," John Seelye argued that Colden was prescient in his *Memoir* as he "stressed both the physical (geopolitical) and spiritual (geopsychological) meaning of what was finally accomplished."

In the larger scheme of things, then, the Erie Canal helped to fulfill the vision of the founding fathers. As a "technological mechanism designed to carry out the geopolitical function of the Constitution—which was to assist in the spread of the Union while ensuring its stability."

In the complete landscape that marked these October days of honor, then, and the many arduous years leading up to them, Lockport had assumed a most important role, and its gala celebration was second to none. Its place in history, and in the pantheon of American towns and cities that had made a unique contribution to the maintenance of the Republic, had been justly earned, and fame and distinction followed.

Many Eyes Focused on Lockport

In the years following the celebration of 1825, Lockport had the eyes of many travelers, both at home and from abroad, focused upon it. It became a major tourist attraction at the same time European visitors flocked to American shores to see how the American experiment in democracy was faring. The most famous of these was Alexis de Tocqueville, who wrote his insightful interpretation of the American nation and character, *Democracy in America*, based upon his tour in the 1830s. Historians are fortunate to have these written accounts of visitors, to the United States in general and to the Erie Canal in particular, which was often part of the itinerary. Many visitors were naturally attracted to the canal and to Niagara Falls, and the "eighth man-made wonder," the Lockport locks, were close by this natural wonder.

Perhaps the most famous commentator on Lockport was the Englishwoman Frances Trollope, who wrote *Domestic Manners of the Americans* in 1832. In an abridged introduction to these volumes, John Lauritz Larson captured the essence of Trollope's analysis: "she reported in frank and stinging anecdotes that instantly offended her American readers and thereby helped confirm her notoriety." Her impressions of Lockport were quite negative. As she traveled along the route of the Erie Canal, she opined that Buffalo was "the queerer looking" of all the "thousand and one towns" she visited in America, "though it is not quite so wild as Lockport." Of Lockport, she wrote that it was "beyond all comparison, the strangest looking place I ever beheld." After a "dismal" night there, she "never felt more out of humour at what the Americans call improvement; it is, in truth, as it now stands, a most hideous place, and gladly did I leave it behind me." Luckily for Lockport's future as a tourist attraction, Trollope's views were not typical.

Most of the nineteenth century travelers who came to Lockport wrote with a sense of awe and wonder of the five-tiered locks. In 1826, a Canadian student crossed the border at New York to see the two places that General LaFayette had immortalized together, and observed along the same lines: "As Niagara Falls are the greatest natural wonder, so Lockport, its locks, and the portion of the Erie Canal adjacent, are considered to be the greatest artificial curiosity in this part of America." Lionel Wyld, in his *Low Bridge! Folklore and the Erie Canal*, offered this quote from a southern traveler in the 1830s: "Here, the great Erie Canal has defied nature, and used it like a toy; lock rises upon lock, and miles are cut in the solid stone," and called the famous "Lockport Five" a world-renowned tourist attraction.

In 1828, Karl Bernhard, Duke of Saxe-Weimar Eisenach in the Netherlands, wrote in his *Travels Through North America* his impressions of Lockport. They offer a stark contrast to those of Trollope:

> At this place the canal is carried over the ridge by five large locks . . . ten in number, being arranged in two parallel rows, so that while the boats ascend in one row, they may descend at the same time in the other. Through this arrangement, the navigation is greatly facilitated, and the whole work, hewn through and surrounded by large rocks, presents an imposing aspect.

Moving from the imposing physical sights, the Duke went on to make some telling observations about the life of the community, judged to be "an extremely interesting place:"

> Several hundred Irishmen were at work. They reside in log huts, built along the canal. They make much money; but they suffer also severely in consequence of the unhealthy climate, especially from fevers, which not infrequently prove fatal. . . . Though at present Lockport appears perfectly wild, yet this appearance will no doubt vanish in the course of four or five years, so that it will present as splendid an appearance as Canandaigua or Rochester.

Rather than despair at Lockport's "wildness" like Trollope, this man appreciated its potential, and his predictions were ultimately quite accurate.

A young student at Union College in Utica, another town on the Erie Canal, traveled to see the sites in Lockport and described them in his *Diary of Jonathan Pierce*. Pierce called the locks "the most stupendous work on the whole Canal . . . looked upon as the most perfect specimen of architecture of the kind . . . in the country." He also noted that the stone came from nearby quarries, pointing to one of the mainstays of early Lockport's economy, and pointed out how the people made optimal use of all the natural advantages at their disposal: "the surplus water of the Canal runs off at the upper level and is carried around the side of the hill supplying numerous mills with water. A cotton factory is now underway or about to be in the lower town." The young man was greatly impressed by the experience of traveling through the cavern made by the canal through the limestone, seeing "the rough perpendicular walls pierced in every part with drill holes used for blasting the rock." He was "astonished at the perseverance, labor and expense it cost," and the resulting supply of water at great height, which was bringing more prosperity to the village.

Many of these eyewitness accounts, in addition to describing the impressive physical structure of the locks, express admiration for the community's enterprising spirit, a microcosmic reflection of what was perceived to be the long term effects and blessings of the Erie Canal. In his *Memoir*, Cadwallader Colden looked to the future as he wrote to preserve the historical record of these unprecedented days in American history:

> The history of the Canals is one of the proudest monuments that the present age will transmit to posterity . . . they exhibit the most impressive example which the United States has yet produced, since the adoption of the Federal Constitution, of the beneficent effects of a free Government, upon the character of a community. They are intimately connected with the best hopes of the Republic.

Another contemporary who indulged in "a boastful disposition in anticipation of future greatness" was Thurlow Weed, aspiring politician and editor of the *Telegraph*, a Rochester newspaper, in 1825. Shortly after the capstone celebration, he referred to the now famous locks as "a work which will probably remain for ages as a monument of American genius and American patriotism."

These contemporary predictions of future greatness, part and parcel of the many superlatives used to describe the Lockport locks and the Erie Canal as a whole, turned out to be an accurate harbinger of the rising economic tide sweeping across the Empire State. In Lockport, there was some concern that the completion of the locks would be something of a let-down in the short run, as fears of people leaving once the work was done would result in the community becoming a ghost town. Fortunately those fears were groundless, as Lockport continued to grow over time and moved on to the next stage of its history, when the economic effects of the canal intersected once again with the community's social and political life. These connections, for both good and ill, elicited a new type of attention focused on Lockport. Prior allusions to the ripple effects of the canal on the spirit of Lockport proved to be all too true. In the words of Frances Trollope, the village would become something of a "battleground" between nature and technology, with the "demon of machinery" taking possession of the town, and additional demons giving rise to new social, political, and religious tensions. The search for harmony, as well as prosperity, was to be continued.

Chapter Five

CURIOUS MANIFESTATIONS OF
BEWILDERING SOCIAL CHANGE

In the United States associations are established to promote the public safety, commerce, industry, morality and religion. There is no end which the human will despairs of attaining through the combined power of individuals united into a society . . . there is scarcely a hamlet that has not its newspaper. It may readily be imagined that neither discipline nor unity of action can be established among so many combatants, and each one consequently fights under his own standard.
—Alexis de Tocqueville, *Democracy in America*, 1835

After the completion of the locks and the grand opening of the Erie Canal in 1825, Lockport secured its place on the map of the United States and in the nation's history. Over the next several decades Lockport's story was part of the larger American one, as the nation struggled through the years leading up to the Civil War. It was a time, in the words of those who lived through it and of the historians who wrote about, of "bewildering social change," exhibited in numerous political, economic, and religious episodes that attracted considerable attention. New York had a particularly important role to play in this drama as the fires of religious revival followed a path along the Erie Canal, which became known as the "burned over district."

As these numerous changes were taking place, Alexis de Tocqueville, observer of all things American, was writing his masterpiece in an attempt to come to grips with and explain, as an outsider, the democratic spirit that defined the nation. In his introduction, he stated that "it is evident to all alike that a great democratic revolution is going on among us, but all do not look at it in the same light." As he traveled he looked for evidence wherever he could find it, and plumbed the depths of the American experience from a variety of perspectives, exploring religion and sects, political associations and parties, and the power of the press in the young republic. Among Tocqueville's most famous lines are these, underscoring the important relationship between religion and politics that prevailed in the United States: "Religion in America takes no direct part in the government of society, but it must be regarded as the first of their political institutions . . . they hold it to be indispensable to the maintenance of republican institutions."

Examples of the truth of this observation can be found in several "curiosities" and "controversies" that arose in Lockport during the late 1820s and 1830s, reflections on a smaller scale of the national drama of revival religion and political tension surrounding the power of the Freemasons that were part and parcel of antebellum America's fascination with reform. From 1828 to 1829, a monthly newspaper was published in Lockport by Lyman Spalding, rising entrepreneur and leading citizen of the village. Its purpose was to expose the threat of "priestcraft," and the unholy alliance of church and state. Lockport also had a prominent role to play in the events surrounding the disappearance of William H. Morgan, a Mason planning to expose the secrets of the organization. The eyes of the entire nation and Canada were riveted on western New York from the time of his disappearance in 1826 through the trials, which started in 1830, of those charged with his kidnapping. His fate remains a mystery to this day. The village where the amazing locks were built achieved a different sort of fame in the decades following the opening of the Erie Canal. It became the scene of some bizarre occurrences, and attracted a sort of attention that might be labeled "infamous," all part of the larger dislocations experienced in America when the forces of religion and politics collided.

Yet even as these events took place, writ large, Lockport was also occupied with its local concerns. In the aftermath of the celebrations marking the completion of the locks and the canal, several thousand canal workers moved on, and the population dropped. But rather than becoming a ghost town, Lockport rebounded, and the state of New York formally incorporated the village in 1829. In addition to establishing a more formal government and municipal organization, such as a board of trustees with Joel McCollum serving as president, there was the continuing process of developing the community's economic, civic, and spiritual life. And it was this process that led to conflict in the course of trying to build consensus and stability.

Lockport's Place in the Larger Scheme of Things

In an early "History of Niagara County" (1878), preserved today in the Local History Room of the Lockport Public Library, the introduction takes up the challenges and benefits of writing local history. Perhaps with the events of the early nineteenth century in mind, the editor notes: "To one whose own neighborhood has been the theatre of events prominent in the nation's annals, the history of these events is the most interesting of all history." Surely this is true of the social and political controversies that defined Lockport in the years after 1825.

Several standard U.S. history monographs mention Lockport's role in the history of antebellum American reform, but give it little more than a passing reference or footnote. Nevertheless, these works provide the necessary context for understanding why Lockport gained notoriety as a result of how it experienced and contributed to the religious tensions accompanying the market revolution that came in the wake of the Erie Canal, and its role in the rise of the anti-Masonic political party, the first "third party" in American history.

Alice Felt Tyler's *Freedom's Ferment: Phases of American Social History from the Colonial Period to the Outbreak of the Civil War* (1944) points to events in Lockport with respect to both the William Morgan trials and the religious revivals, or second great awakening, which shook many of the towns along the canal. Her purpose is to demonstrate that the "religious movements and adventures in reform" including anti-slavery and temperance—which were also evident in Lockport—had a "profound and permanent effect on American civilization." Along with the more well-known crusades and reforms, she argued, "the eccentricities of the era have had more than their due share of the limelight." Occasionally, this "restless ferment," a symptom of the "dynamic democracy" that Alexis de Tocqueville found so fascinating, could also have a darker side. Nativism and bigotry blossomed in organized movements that targeted Catholics and Mormons as well as Masons, accusing these groups of being un-American and denying democratic principles. These spasmodic outpourings of fear and prejudice stemmed from the "perplexities of a nation" in the throes of unprecedented change, good and bad. Another historian, David Brion Davis, analyzed "Anti-Masonic, Anti-Catholic, and Anti-Mormon Literature" in a 1960 article on "Some Themes of Counter-Subversion," and concluded that fears of internal subversion were channeled into a number of powerful counter movements, evoking images of enemies of American freedom and democracy and conspiracies that threatened republican virtues and values.

The village of Lockport was experiencing great changes, which were perceived as posing a threat to the same republican virtues and values that had been celebrated at the time of the dedication of the locks. In lashing out at religious sects that promoted "priestcraft," or being torn between defending their neighbors who were Masons or jumping on the bandwagon of the anti-Masonic movement, some of the citizens of Lockport exhibited signs of the confusion and madness that characterized these heady times.

Another current of change, associated most directly with the path of the Erie Canal running through western New York, expressed itself in the form of religious "enthusiasm." Historian Whitney Cross wrote the seminal work on this subject in 1950: *The Burned-Over District: The Social and Intellectual History of Enthusiastic Religion in Western New York, 1800–1850.* Arguing that the subject of religion had a broader significance than might first be apparent for this period of American history, Cross delineated western New York as the "storm center" of the religious forces that were the "driving propellants" of social movements, and referred to the "line of DeWitt Clinton's famed canal" as a "psychic highway": "Upon it congregated a people extraordinarily given to unusual religious beliefs, peculiarly devoted to crusades aimed at the perfection of mankind, and the attainment of millennial happiness."

Characterizing Lockport as a new community that "rapidly became the major town between Rochester and Buffalo," Cross also noted that among canal towns, Lockport was "warm," rather than a genuine hotbed of religious tension. Nevertheless, Lockport went through a multitude of specific changes described by Cross, many of which were motivated by economic and social interests, caught up in a vortex of religious and political strife. These included antislavery and temperance, as well as the more prominent Anti-masonry that looms large in the town's early history (and has a special cabinet devoted to it in the Local History Room of the Public Library).

In a chapter on "Yorker Benevolence," Cross points to four benevolent movements that experienced sudden growth in western New York, and generated a good deal of controversy as well. The issues were the circulation of the Bible, the founding of Sunday schools, the encouragement of temperance, and the enforcement of Sabbath observance, also known as the "Sabbatarian movement." As a result, the region "specialized in argumentative local journals" and newspapers that sought to "mold public opinion." A preponderance of these publications, often short-lived, were founded in Lockport during the 1820s and 1830s. One that covered all of the issues, in a very heated style, is probably Lockport's most fascinating yet hitherto unexplored newspaper, published for two years under the intriguing title *Priestcraft Exposed and Primitive Christianity Defended.*

Priestcraft Exposed and Primitive Christianity Defended

The confusion surrounding this publication stems from its status as an infrequent and inaccurate footnote in books such as Tyler's and a 1938 volume on "the origins of American nativism"—Ray Allen Billington's *The Protestant Crusade*. Both monographs mention publications called "Priestcraft Exposed," in both Concord, New Hampshire and in Lockport. Both the title and context in which they are mentioned lead the reader to assume that the publications were mainly anti-Catholic in sentiment, but this was not the case in Lockport's version. There are traces of anti-Catholicism, of course, as this was a prevailing sentiment in many canal towns, focused first on the Irish who came to dig them and subsequently on the waves of immigrants from Germany and Italy. But the key to understanding Lockport's paper is found by looking at it through the letters and manuscripts of its founder, Lyman A. Spalding.

The specific reasons for the origin and demise of the newspaper are difficult to ascertain, though Cross does make reference to the cry of "Priestcraft!" sounded in the burned over district, by those alarmed at a perceived plot by certain religious sects to impose their beliefs on others and establish a unity of church and state. Spalding, in a series of reminiscences on how he came to settle in Lockport, writes of his own religious odyssey as he traveled from Geneva and Canandaigua. Like many men of his generation, he followed a spiritual path of multiple stops. His father rented a pew for the family in the Presbyterian Church in Geneva, but his paternal uncles belonged to the Universalist and Baptist churches. In 1812, his Aunt Ann Allen "joined the friends, opening the door to Father's acquaintance." In Lockport he boarded with Quakers and became a member, thus joining the company of the Lockport "establishment." He also became a Mason, like many of the prominent members of the business community— seeing no contradiction between membership in the religious Society of Friends and the fraternal organization of Freemasonry.

Spalding referred to his initiation into the world of publishing when he described his role as a joint editor of a small paper in Canandaigua in 1820. Called the *Plain Truth*, it attacked the "schemes of Calvinists to convert the world to Calvinism . . . it had a great run and continued for two years." The same bias was a major motivation for founding *Priestcraft Exposed* in Lockport in 1828, after establishing himself as a business and civic leader in his adopted home. It also ran for two years, and enjoyed a respectable circulation. It appears that Spalding's motives were a mixture of both personal and religious conviction, and financial profit and opportunity, as newspapers devoted to religious controversies were very popular.

The observations by Whitney Cross about Quakers demonstrates that Lockport would be a hospitable home for such a paper: "Quakers did not share the state of mind engendered by the revivalism of the other religious groups" and they had no professional clergy and were not considered "denominational." Letters and manuscripts from the Lyman A. Spalding Collection at the Cornell University Library indicate that one of his major purposes was elucidating for his readers the essential differences between Christianity and Sectarianism, and how the essential teachings of "primitive" Christianity, as outlined in the scriptures, were threatened by sects hungry for political power. "Christianity vs. Sectarianism" is a major theme of his editorials, and letters to his friends explaining the thinking behind the newspaper.

In the context of this heated clash, the definition of the "nefarious mantle of priestcraft" could be found: a body of men called priests had as their objective the making of money, and keeping people ignorant and "enslaved." This "dark force" was threatening the essential truths of Christianity, and *Priestcraft Exposed* was dedicated to defending the foundation and pillars of truth. Spalding lamented the rising tide of "faith without good works," and those who focused on the non-essentials, chastising men to "join the visible church and pay the priest and put on a Sunday face." This tide, he said, created dissension and schism, and detracted from the true value of religion and the promotion of virtuous conduct. Spalding and his paper resorted to labeling their opponents as "notorious cut-throats," "wolves in sheep's clothing," and "hypocrites," preying on the ignorant for their own selfish ends—as they claimed to be on the side of morality, defending true virtue and republican values while sounding a clarion call to "Look to Your Liberties, Americans!"

The masthead of the paper featured a quotation from the Book of Rvelations (XIII, 4), regarding worshipping "the beast" and warnings about the threat posed by *priestcraft*: "was there ever such a craft as priestcraft? No, it is the craftiest of all crafts! It is so crafty that it obtains by its craft the means to make craftsmen, and then it makes the deluded support them." Openly stating its goal as a matter of "Hear Both Sides and Then Judge," the new publication opined that it would serve the interests of the community by offering a forum for discussion, as well as reporting on religious news, both local and regional. A review of its contents from June of 1828 through October of 1829 reveals that it was mired in controversy from the outset, and its tone was one of accusation and denials, attack and counter attack, vituperative language and invective. In an editorial asking for a "fair and impartial hearing," the editor informed his readers:

> Since the publication of our first number, we have been cruelly slandered and accused of opposing *all* religion! We deny this flatly . . . unless religion is synonymous with priestcraft. . . . By PRIEST, we mean all who take up teaching the doctrines of sectarianism as *trade*, and not from a sense of duty . . . CRAFT applies to such as get wealth in their vocation by their craft . . .

a man who is cunning enough to make money by teaching dogmas must be considered a crafty man . . . we oppose these vagabonds, pious frauds and holy lying . . . because we advocate the cause of the indigent and laborious poor against the systematic attacks of the harpies who would fain devour them. . . . We are accused of opposing the spread of the Gospel. . . . Now it is the defence of the Gospel that we think we have undertaken . . . we consider it the duty of every well-wisher to Christianity, virtue and happiness to oppose vice, idleness and priestcraft . . . in what matter is society benefited by those who teach dogmas that have no connection with virtuous practice?

In response to his critics, then, publisher Spalding sought the moral high ground by arguing that he was the defender of true Christianity and virtue, in the interests of promoting happiness and societal well-being. *Priestcraft Exposed* consistently claimed to be an advocate of the cause of freedom, in keeping with the spirit of rational religion and liberal principles—as opposed to proselytizing "priests" who sought to impose their interpretation of religion on the community.

The major preoccupation of the paper, as apparent in the first issues, was its vehement opposition to those who accepted money for preaching the Gospel. It targeted presbyterians and calvinists, and depicted them as "ecclesiastical tyrants" who were hungry for power, both political and religious. As the forces of religion and politics converged in the crisis-ridden atmosphere of the 1820s and 1830s, the stage was set for division and discord. The very future of the community and the nation were at stake. In Lockport, there seemed to be an underlying tension between the two groups who dominated the village in its early days, the Quakers and the Presbyterians.

This concern was not unique to the pages of this publication. In an 1850 *Pioneer History*, the memory of certain pioneer Christian ministers was honored—those who "returning to their homes after thus itinerating, labored with their hands, that they might not be chargeable upon the brethren." But from 1828 through 1829, *Priestcraft Exposed* led the charge against the "serpentine" scoundrels who sought to make money as they ostensibly "preached." Its pages are a compendium of religious prejudices. In the process of exposing the local presbyterians, readers were reminded of the horrors of the Spanish Inquisition and the ignorant Irish Catholics, oppressed and persecuted by their own priests who took from them "their own bread," in order to "evangelize and enslave East Indians." There are numerous anti-Catholic and anti-Semitic references, as if depicting the presbyterians in the same company with Catholics or Jews was seen as a most effective way of undermining support for them. In the idiom of the day, "jesuitical" was an effective slur, as presbyterian clergy were likened to "the jesuits of America" in their campaign to become a "national clergy." There were several arguments to the effect that "we aver the institution of the Sabbath is wholly Jewish," and that one cannot find sound scriptural support for Sunday as the commonly accepted Sabbath.

This reference to the Sabbath highlights one of the greatest controversies of that place and time—"Sabbatarianism." There was a constant refrain of opposition to the notion of "blue laws," or lobbying for laws to prevent people from conducting business on Sundays. The specific target was the "Pioneer Line" of stages and boats, founded for the purpose of respecting the Sabbath.

Here, the claims of religious observance, as interpreted by some members of the community, collided with those who wished to carry on their business enterprises on Sunday, with no disrespect for religious principles implied or intended. To the editor of *Priestcraft Exposed,* it was a matter of freedom, and not allowing one group in the community to impose its standards on the rest. Pointing out the absurdities of those who compared breaking the Sabbath with truly heinous crimes, the paper wrote anecdotally of many instances that supported their position: a minister who said that Sabbath breaking was worse than murder, or another who had the audacity to condemn President John Quincy Adams and President-elect Andrew Jackson for traveling on Sunday. Many articles, with titles like "Religion in Boats," "Sabbatarian Zeal," and "Sunday Police" reinforced the notion that those who insisted on their definition of Sunday observance were elitist and intolerant. These "powerful sects" that sought to force the abstinence from labor one day a week were the same ones that held the idea that "worship and prayer can only be performed in an assembly with a priest to direct the ceremonies." This idea was seen as both "superstitious and anti-christian." The issue of "Sabbatarianism" was one causing trouble in many communities, and the paper reprinted stories from other towns and states. The exaggerated charges made in an article from the *Boston Patriot* were fairly typical. Contrary to those "Sunday policemen" who would impose their views on others and exact civil penalties in the process were the pious men who respected freedom:

> True piety is retired, modest and diffident of Itself; it is the very reverse of the dogmatical, overbearing and inquisitional spirit of persecution . . . what reason can be given then, for using this force, that it will not apply with equal justice in favor of Catholics enforcing Protestants an abstinence from meat during Lent, and in favor of Mahometans compelling Christians to worship Mahomet?

Clearly, from the perspective of the editor, the stakes in this struggle were very high. Other histories of Lockport and Niagara County have dealt with the issue of Sunday "blue laws" and the opposition to them in the village, especially when it came to practical matters like mail delivery and businesses being allowed to operate. A History of Niagara County published in 1878 noted that the question produced considerable discord and dissension in Lockport. The "Pioneer Line" was started specifically to be a "lever of sufficient power" to prevail over the "seven day mail traffic," for "preaching prevailed not" in the clamor for reform. A great many of the "most prominent citizens" were strongly opposed to discontinuing mail delivery on Sundays, and called a meeting to "remonstrate" against it on December 9, 1828—when Spalding's publication had reached a fever pitch on the subject. It was well-attended, and resulted in a petition signed by many, including the "owners of prominent mercantile establishments." On the other side, a Deacon John Gooding, one of the stockholders in the Pioneer Line, resided at Washington and Gooding Streets, where the stages stopped for repairs at a local blacksmith's—the neighborhood was known thereafter, according to local lore, as "pioneer hill." Eventually the Pioneer Line, "without accomplishing the object for which it was started" or proving to be a "paying investment," closed up its business and withdrew from the field. Propaganda and political organization employed in the cause of opposing the Sabbatarians had prevailed.

Other issues of grave concern that found their way into the pages of Lockport's monthly paper included Sunday schools, the support of missionaries, Bible and Tract Societies, and fears of a general plot to impose a union of church and state upon the good citizens of Lockport. In the summer of 1828 the editor announced: "let sound Presbyterians understand that this country cannot be brought under their influence by means of Sunday schools . . . the friends of religious freedom and liberal discussion are not so weak as to believe the presbyterians strong enough at the moment to subvert our religious liberties."

Warning that "the march of Kingcraft and Priestcraft—of temporal and spiritual tyranny—is slow, but generally has been sure," the editorial went on to declare "we are hostile to the deep laid plan of inculcating peculiar sectarian tenets of religion, under the guise of Sunday Schools. A letter to the editor signed "Millennarian" boldly stated that benevolent societies were a "subterfuge to draw the minds of the people insensibly along to the adoption of an established religion, with an orthodox national creed . . . government will become altogether ecclesiastical." The implication—that the freedoms won during the American Revolution and enshrined by the founding fathers in the Constitution were in danger—was quite clear.

In addition to these generalized exhortations to be on guard against the subversion of liberty by the forces of "sectarian" religion, the paper drew attention to the dangers closer to home in relaying the story of another instance of "deplorable bigotry:"

> In the village of Lockport, individuals of the most unexceptional moral character have been publicly excommunicated by the *Priest* of the Presbyterian church, for changing their religious sentiments. In other sections of the country, individuals have like-wise been deprived of their civil rights, on account of their opinions not being "orthodox."

The alarm was repeatedly sounded against the elements of this organized conspiracy of "Clerical Power" and despotism, noting that the pages of European history were blackened with their crimes—"Catholic or Protestant, Episcopalian or Presbyterian."

If one purpose of Spalding's paper was to stir up controversy, it was succeeding. The Lockport publication often engaged in a war of words with a "presbyterian" paper from a neighboring community, the *Rochester Observer*. To Spalding, it was noteworthy for its "dogmatical and arrogant spirit," while his paper, of course, stood for truth. An issue of contention between them was that of missionaries, who were begging for money to convert "heathen Indians and Catholics." According to *Priestcraft Exposed*, these missionary societies were motivated mainly by their search for revenue, which they often squandered once they obtained it: too many of the funds raised went to pay the exorbitant salaries of the priests, or were used to run seminaries, sometimes depicted as "priest-producing enterprises." As the contest between the papers heated up, other papers took note of the rivalry and counter charges. To his credit, Lyman Spalding acknowledged and printed these criticisms of his own paper. An Albany publication stated that the principal object of *Priestcraft Exposed* appeared to be "the abuse of the *Rochester Observer*," and reminded its readers that "some years ago, Lockport was familiarly known by the name of Sodom!" The level of invective in this conflict knew no bounds.

The Lockport paper called those associated with the Rochester paper "Calvinistic freaks," who were "endeavoring to gain political ascendancy in this country" and were motivated by "sectarian ambition and party proselytism." Defending itself against the charges of these people, the subscribers to *Priestcraft Exposed* were reminded that "Jesus himself was crucified by the orthodox of his day!" Spalding reprinted a stark criticism of his paper in November of 1828 that claimed *Priestcraft Exposed's* "appalling and unholy sign" in front of its offices was a disgrace to Lockport. Another presbyterian paper referred to the "vile production issued at Lockport" as an "infidel paper." Over time, Spalding would build alliances between his paper and others of the same type, and even print notices that his offices would receive subscriptions to the *Free Meetings Advocate* of Auburn, New York and the *Plain Truth* of Rochester. This type of networking, seeking strength in numbers, was seen as essential as the number of newspapers escalated and everyone chose sides on the many controversial issues of the day.

In 1829, Spalding offered perspective on his decision to keep the paper going for another year in an editorial entitled "Proposals for Publishing Volume II." It provides the best summary insight into his motivations for starting the paper, and indirectly, for his decision to close the paper later that year, perhaps because the Pioneer Line folded. Spalding continued to harangue against Rochestarian Josiah Bissell's "Pioneer Stages" as the proprietor arrogantly boasted that he would sustain the business at all costs, contending that it was the "cause of God" and must be supported. Spalding suggested that contributions collected in Presbyterian churches were a main source of his support, and that Bissell had set up the stages and boats as "instruments of moral suasion." He asked whether an "intelligent community could be successfully hoodwinked" or whether it would wake up in response to the warnings of *Priestcraft Exposed*.

Spalding reminded his readers that he had been forced to defend himself against charges that he was an atheist and went on in later issues to expound upon his own chosen beliefs, those of the Society of Friends. He recommended the Quakers as a community "organized on the most liberal of principles" and consistently opposed to "sectarian despots." Stating that it was "an ardent desire to aid in protecting the liberties of the people against the systematic attacks of the Orthodox Priesthood" that led him to start the paper, it now "induces the Editor of this work to propose its continuance for another year. . . . We did not undertake this publication for any sectarian purpose, nor for stigmatizing any particular sect." He had tried to stand up for both truth and genuine religion—he hoped, with considerable success—and congratulated his readers, for "the attempts of the Pioneer to obtain the mail have proved abortive." Resolving to carry on the good fight for another year, he invited his "well informed" readers to continue their support of his efforts to uphold the "essentials of Christianity" characterized by a "disposition to seek that which is honest, and to lead a virtuous and upright life."

Although the life of *Priestcraft Exposed and Primitive Christianity Defended* was relatively short, it serves as a valuable source to demonstrate that the town of Lockport was part of the wild mainstream that constituted American society during the era of reform and religious enthusiasm. Its pages also carried notices of local meetings for temperance and anti-slavery. At times, given the contentious atmosphere that prevailed in the burned over district, the controversies that engaged the citizens of Lockport became very hot. Spalding experienced some difficulty maintaining his balance on the moral high ground, for his tendency to resort to name-calling, like that of his opponents, led both sides in some troublesome directions—all reflective of the spirit of the times. Spalding's reputation as a civil and business leader no doubt helped preserve his good standing in the community. All of the locals engaged in the high profile case of William Morgan's disappearance and the subsequent rise of Anti-Masonry, on the other hand, would not be as fortunate.

The Mysterious Case of William Morgan and the Anti-Masonic Movement

The disappearance of William Morgan during the era of antebellum reform, religious enthusiasm, and even a little madness brought Lockport into the national limelight once again, a year after its famous locks were acclaimed as American's greatest engineering feat. In 1826, however, the attention was not so favorable, as some of Lockport's most prominent citizens were put on trial for crimes surrounding this most bizarre episode. Unlike some of the other issues that merited mention of a mere connection to events, such as religious revivalism or abolitionism, Lockport was close to the center of this story rather than on the periphery.

Most historical accounts of the Morgan affair focus on it as the strangest of episodes, shrouded in mystery, secrecy, and clandestine plots, which gave birth to the anti-Masonic political party. For the town of Lockport, the ensuing conflict between the fraternal order of Freemasonry and a movement dedicated to eradicating its power in American life struck at the very heart of the community and its sense of law and order. And it engendered a new wave of factionalism throughout western New York, as Masonry's supporters and foes battled in the moral, political, and economic marketplaces of many canal towns.

As was readily apparent in all the festivities celebrating the opening of the Erie Canal, the Masons were well-established in Lockport. The town's lodge was one of the oldest in western New York, and counted among its membership most of Lockport's business and civic leaders, who met regularly at the Niagara Hotel. Until the notorious case of Morgan, the Masonic order had always served the needs of the community well. After the furor subsided, the Lockport Masons managed to reconstitute themselves and remain a viable and valued organization in the town, but their reputation would always be colored by the outrageous plot of 1826.

Both Alice Felt Tyler and Whitney Cross, who devote considerable attention to the Morgan case in their monographs, suggest that it was "no coincidence" that the anti-Masonic movement grew out of the tempestuous times and events associated with the burned over district. The attack on Masons after 1827, according to Tyler, was "social and economic in origin, but largely political in its expression . . . an extraordinary manifestation of the combination of principle, prejudice and hysteria that has often confounded students of American democracy." Cross places the movement in the larger historical stream:

> Which glides in a smooth current for a time, until certain forces, gathering in
> a brewing storm, break forth to ruffle the surface and alter the direction of the
> flow. Some dramatic event or masterful man, a product of the accumulating
> tokens of change, then sets off the reservoir of energy which whips the stream
> to turbulence.

This metaphorical image is a most appropriate description of the agitation that seized Lockport and many surrounding communities, as the disappearance of a "Mason turned traitor" had all the elements of a great drama. Cross, in fact, analyzes the case of "The Martyr" as one of a number of "catalytic agents," such as the arrival and "galvanizing effects" of the Erie Canal, and the religious revivals of Charles Grandison Finney, which released their "dynamic influence" across western New York.

Trying to discover the incontrovertible facts about the Morgan case is not an easy task, as a story this convoluted and mired in secrecy is bound to be confusing. Some basic facts, however, have been common in most historical accounts, and the most detailed and lengthy record of the Morgan affair, as it pertains to Lockport, can be found in a 1966 pamphlet written by Clarence O. Lewis, Niagara County historian. Lewis concluded his 32 page typescript with these words on behalf of its authenticity and reliability: "this history . . . is the result of sixty years of research and, I believe, is as accurate [an] account as can ever be written." There is a good deal of truth to his claim, though it should be noted that Lewis was not without his own bias, obviously favorable to the Masons.

William Morgan, a stonemason by trade, suffered considerable economic hardship after moving from Virginia to find work in Canada and New York. Like many a man trying to make his way into society, he knew the value of becoming a Mason, in a state where over half the office holders belonged to the organization that wielded considerable influence in economic, social, and political affairs. In New York, he moved from the town of Porter in Niagara County to Rochester. Although he frequented several lodges, he had trouble fitting in for lack of sponsors and never advanced beyond the first "Royal Arch" degree. His petition to join the chapter at Batavia was turned down when one of the members crossed out his name or "black-balled" him. This was the most likely reason for the resentment and disaffection that led him to write an exposé of the order. Lewis opens his account with a bit of conspiracy theory of his own, thus revealing his own subjectivity:

Continued on page 97

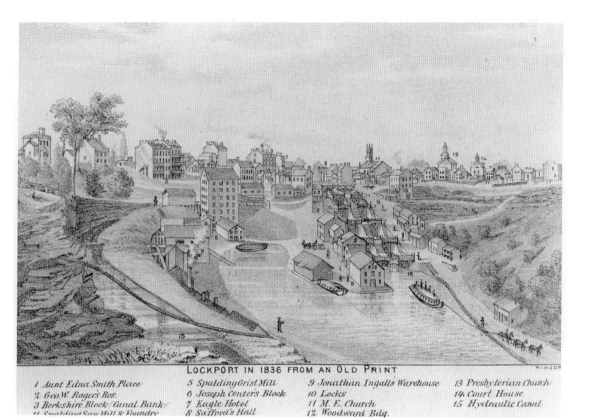

LOCKPORT IN 1836 FROM AN OLD PRINT

WINSOR

1 Aunt Edna Smith Place	5 Spalding Grist Mill	9 Jonathan Ingalls Warehouse	13 Presbyterian Church
2 Geo.W. Rogers Res.	6 Joseph Center's Block	10 Locks	14 Court House
3 Berkshire Block (Canal Bank)	7 Eagle Hotel	11 M. E. Church	15 Hydraulic Canal
4 Spalding Saw Mill & Foundry	8 Safford's Hall	12 Woodward Bdg.	

VIEW OF THE UPPER VILLAGE OF LOCKPORT. This 1836 print is one of the earliest representations of early Lockport, the seat of Niagara County, New York. The drawing by W. Wilson highlights prominent landmarks such as Aunt Ednah Smith's home, the Presbyterian Church, and Lyman Spalding's mills. A lithograph by J. H. Buford of the same scene is one of the most frequently reproduced scenes of Lockport in the "pioneer" days. (Lockport Public Library, Polster Collection.)

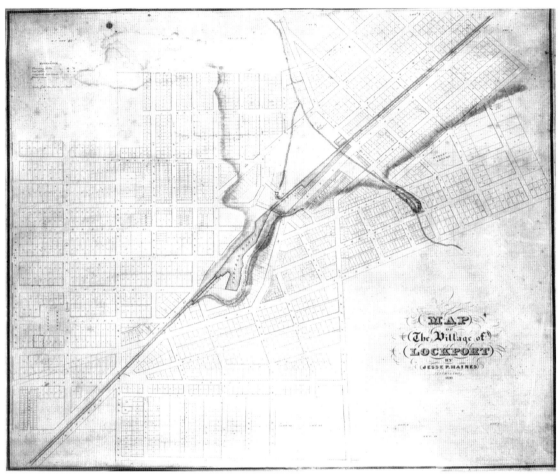

1830 MAP OF THE VILLAGE OF LOCKPORT. Jesse Haines produced the first known map of Lockport in 1830, featuring the canal running through the heart of the village and taking note of the street names already in place. (Lockport Public Library, Polster Collection.)

COMBINED LOCKS ON THE ERIE CANAL AT LOCKPORT. This print of the famous locks at Lockport appeared in the Harper's New Monthly Magazine *in 1880.*

BOAT AGAINST THE BACKDROP OF THE LOCKPORT LOCKS. A common scene in Lockport, central to the community's economic health—one of hundreds of boats which "sailed uphill" along the path of its canal journey in the late nineteenth century. (Author's collection.)

TOWPATH VIEW. From the perspective of the towpath, another view of the canal and the locks. (Author's collection.)

COLONEL WILLIAM BOND HOUSE, 143 ONTARIO STREET. This home built by one of Lockport's prominent first citizens (and land speculators) in 1824 was the first brick home in Lockport. It is now on the National Register of historic sites, and forms part of the complex of buildings at the Niagara County Historical Society. (Brent Merrill photograph.)

FIRST PRESBYTERIAN CHURCH. One of Lockport's first churches, this church started out as a log cabin in 1823. Since that time, it has been reconstructed several times, and now occupies a site, appropriately enough, on Church Street.(Lockport Public Library files.)

PULPIT.

ORGAN

The Seats will be rented on the 29th day of
December, 1884, at 2 o'clock P. M.

83 $10	$12 59	20 $12	60 $12	$10 94
81 $22	$12 57	19 $18	58 $12	$22 92
89 $24	$26.50 55	18 $25	56 $26.50	$34 90
87 $24	$12 53	17 $45	54 $42	$24 88
85 $32	$12 51	16 $90	52 $42	$32 86
84 $45	$30 49	15 $100	50 $50	$45 84
81 $45	$75 47	14 $100	48 $75	$45 82
79 $35	$90 45	13 $100	46 $90	$35 80
77 $40	$75 43	12 Reserved	44 $75	$40 78
75 $40	$50 41	11 $100	42 $50	$40 76
73 $35	$65 39	10 $100	40 $45	$35 74
71 $30	$50 37	9 $90	38 $45	$25 72
69 $32	$50 35	8 70	36 $45	$20 70
67 $34	$30 33	7 $90	34 $35	$18 68
65 $25	$12 31	6 $45	32 $30	$12 66
63 $15	$30 29	5 $40	30 $20	$10 64
61 $15	$25 27	4 $30	28 $10	$5 62
26 $15	$30 25	3 $30		
24 $20	$10 23	2 $30		
22 $10	$15 21	1 $30		

PEW RENTAL CHART. A common practice at many nineteenth century churches was the rental of pews. A family, according to its financial means, would secure a place not only in the church but in the community hierarchy. This document from 1884 indicates prices at Lockport's Congregational Church. (Lockport Public Library files.)

CONSTRUCTION "CREW" OF ST. PATRICK'S CHURCH. The second Catholic Church in Lockport was St. Patrick's, named in honor of the Irish saint. This photo features Monsignior Cannon, pastor, with a crew of immigrant stone masons who built and remodeled the church.

ST. JOHN'S ROMAN CATHOLIC CHURCH. *St. John's was the first Catholic Parish/Church established in Lockport. This structure was one of the reconstructed versions of the building on Chestnut Street. It was replaced by the current building in the 1970s. (Lockport Public Library files.)*

PATRICK'S ROMAN CATHOLIC CHURCH. *A contemporary view of the edifice of St. Patrick's Church, located at 76 Church Street, Lockport. (Emily Riley photograph.)*

JESSE HAWLEY HISTORIC MARKER. This New York State Historic marker on Cold Springs Road in the town of Lockport draws attention to the final resting place of the man credited with devising the idea of a canal in his "Hercules" essays. (Brent Merrill photograph.)

QUAKER CEMETERY AT HARTLAND. Located on the Ridge Road outside of Lockport, in the Niagara County town of Hartland, this historic sign marks the place where the Quaker community established an early burial ground.

CHURCH STREET. An early postcard focusing on the "Christian enterprise of vast proportions" established on Church Street in Lockport, with its ecumenical mix of steeples.

LOCKPORT UNION SCHOOL
Thoroughly up-to-date school, which has its own library

UNION SCHOOL BUILDING. This 1890s building housed the Union School of Lockport, the first such school system in the state of New York and a harbinger of public secondary education in the United States. (Lockport Public Library files.)

DEWITT CLINTON SCHOOL. Named in honor of the governor who worked tirelessly to bring his dream of the Erie Canal to fruition, this school was built in 1925 on Clinton Street, in the heart of Lockport's Lowertown. It remains one of the finest elementary schools in the Lockport school system, staffed by dedicated veteran teachers like Mrs. Molly Castle Peer. (Lockport Public Library, Polster Collection.)

OLD LOCKPORT/NIAGARA COUNTY JAIL. Built in 1844, this building (and its earlier renditions) was associated with several famous nineteenth century trials,including the Morgan-Masonic case and the "McLeod episode" in the Patriot War. (Lockport Public Library, Polster Collection.)

UNION STATION. This historic building was the site of the railroad station/depot of the New York Central in Lockport, built in 1887. Several attempts to revive and renovate it after it was destroyed by fire were undertaken by Lockport citizens with mixed success, and the last restoration project was ultimately cancelled—a significant loss of a treasured piece of Lockport's past. (Lockport Public Library, Polster Collection.)

WASHINGTON HUNT LAW OFFICE. The only governor of New York state to come from Niagara County, Hunt's original law office in Lockport is recognized for its historic significance, and is now part of the complex of the Niagara County Historical Society buildings. (Brent Merrill photograph.)

The Original I. O. O. F. Home, Lockport, N. Y.

ODD FELLOWS HOME. This old photograph depicts the original Odd Fellows home, one of early Lockport's civic and charitable establishments. It has undergone many changes over the years, but still exists as a rest/nursing home facility in the town.

HISTORIC SITE OF COUNTY CLERK'S OFFICE. As the Niagara County Historic site marker indicates, this building served as the original site of the county clerk's office, across the street from the present day courthouse. It now serves as the county historian's office. (Emily Riley photograph.)

NIAGARA COUNTY COURT HOUSE. As the seat of Niagara County, New York, Lockport is the site of all the county's official buildings, gathered in the block now bordered by Niagara Street, Hawley Street, and Park Place. (Lockport Public Library, Polster Collection.)

HODGE OPERA HOUSE. This photo shows the historic Hodge Opera House in ruins, destroyed by a second tragic fire in 1928. On its foundation, the Bewley Building was constructed, and still exists at the corner of Market and Main Streets in the city of Lockport. (Lockport Public Library, Polster Collection.)

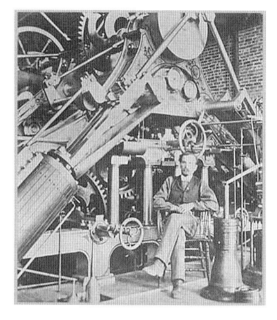

BIRDSILL HOLLY. Once described by the Buffalo Courier-Express as "Lockport's Legend," Birdsill Holly was a prolific inventor, most notably of the fire hydrant protection system and the district steam heating system. His Holly Manufacturing Company on the hydraulic raceway brought prosperity and fame to the city.

HOLLY PUMP. This photo of one of Holly's water pumps was featured in a prominent display of inventors at the Smithsonian Institution.

WEDDING OF THE WATERS. A replica of a famous painting of Governor Dewitt Clinton performing the historic "wedding of the waters" ceremony to commemorate the official opening of the Erie Canal in 1825, this photo was taken at the Canal Museum at the foot of the locks. (Brent Merrill photograph.)

SURVIVING ORIGINAL LOCKS.
This contemporary snapshot of the surviving original locks at Lockport—replaced by the two Locks #34 and #35 in the Barge Canal System—demonstrates that they still function as a means of surplus water flow in Lockport today. (Brent Merrill photograph.)

THE BIG BRIDGE. This historic marker draws attention to the fact that Lockport's "Big Bridge" was renowned as one of the widest bridges in the world, built over the canal. (Brent Merrill photograph.)

RICHMOND AVENUE AT THE BIG BRIDGE. This historic photograph taken at a crossroads in downtown Lockport illustrates the vibrant business and community life, against the background of the community's very visible church steeples. (Lockport Public Library, Polster Collection.)

MARKET ON LOCKPORT'S BIG BRIDGE. Taken in the dead of winter, this photo depicts the busy marketplace at the Big Bridge in the heart of Lockport. (Lockport Public Library, Polster Collection.)

OLD CITY HALL. The "Old City Hall" on the Pine Street Bridge over the canal in Lockport has been maintained as a historic building, and served as the location of a variety of businesses, including restaurants, over the years. (Lockport Public Library, Polster Collection.)

MARKET STREET. This classic photo/postcard depicts a very busy commercial district in Lockport, in the year 1912.

"UPSIDE DOWN" RAILROAD BRIDGE. An old photograph of the Lockport curiosity and landmark that remains something of a tourist attraction today. (Lockport Public Library, Polster Collection.)

EXCHANGE STREET BRIDGE. This tunnel/bridge on Exchange Street looks down toward Lowertown, and appears to be carved out of the escarpment rock formation. (Lockport Public Library, Polster Collection.)

EXCHANGE STREET LIFT BRIDGE. One of two lift bridges still in operation over the Canal in Lockport, this contemporary photograph features the bridge lifted up to allow the boat to safely pass through on its way up the canal. (Brent Merrill photograph.)

ADAMS STREET BRIDGE. Another bridge, located along the canal in the Lowertown Section of Lockport, raised to allow another boat to continue on its journey along the canal. (Brent Merrill photograph.)

DeSALES STONE HOUSE. This old stone house on Chestnut Ridge Road in Lockport was incorporated into the building known as DeSales Catholic High School, which graduated its first class of young men in 1950. It served as the residence of the Oblates of St. Francis DeSales who taught at DeSales, and is part of the building that now serves as DeSales Catholic School, the only surviving parochial school in Lockport today. (Emily Riley photograph.)

CANAL MUSEUM. Located at the foot of the locks, this little museum in Lockport features artifacts from the construction of and travel on the canal. (Emily Riley photograph.)

HISTORIC PALACE THEATRE. This contemporary photo depicts the Palace Theatre on East Avenue in Lockport, recently restored and revived by community efforts to bring entertainment and culture back to the downtown area. (Emily Riley photograph.)

LOCKPORT MEMORIAL HOSPITAL. Lockport's hospital, first constructed in 1908. It has been expanded and renovated many times since then, and still serves as the community's hospital on East Avenue. (Lockport Public Library files.)

LOWERTOWN HISTORIC DISTRICT.
This plaque describes the place of Lowertown
in Lockport's history, and is indicative of
the successful community efforts to recognize
and preserve this district and many of its fine
buildings. (Brent Merrill photograph.)

GRIMBLE'S HARDWARE
FAÇADE. This recently painted and
decorated back view of one of Lockport's
long-established businesses was
photographed from one of the Lockport
cruise boats on the canal, part of a
renaissance in tourism currently underway
in the city.

LOCKVIEW IV CRUISE BOAT. One of
Mike Murphy's Lockport Locks and Erie
Canal Cruises boats, featured on the History
Channel's Modern Marvels *program. (Brent*
Merrill photograph.)

WIDEWATER MARINA. This view of the Widewater Marina depicts one of the widest areas on the Erie Canal, traditionally allowing boats to turn around and change direction on the canal. Today, Widewater's is the location of a canal walkway and park, and the scene of community events like the annual Barbara Ennis Memorial Walk. (Brent Merrill photograph.)

THE 100th MILESTONE. This drawing by local artist Joe Whalen appeared on the editorial page of the special edition of the Union-Sun & Journal *newspaper printed on July 17, 1965 to commemorate the centennial of the City of Lockport. (Lockport Public Library files.)*

HARRISON RADIATOR PLANT. This building was the engineering center and factory of the company founded by Herbert Champion Harrison in 1910. Although no longer part of the Delphi-Harrison Corporation, Lockport's largest employer (operations have shifted to the west plant on the outskirts of town), the building remains standing on Walnut Street in the city. (Lockport Public Library, Polster Collection.)

HARRISON RADIATOR COMMEMORATIVE BOOKLET. This cover of a commemorative booklet about Lockport's largest industry indicates that it was essential to the economic health of the community. (Lockport Public Library files.)

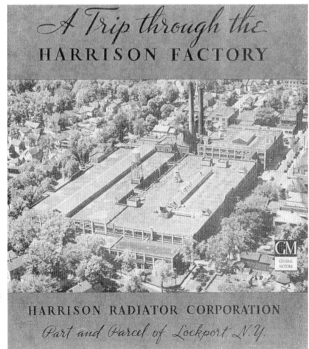

GOLDWATER-MILLER TICKET. *This photograph features the Republican presidential and vice-presidential candidates in 1964: Arizona senator Barry Goldwater and New York congressman William E. Miller. Lockport took great pride in its favorite son rising to national prominence despite the fact that the ticket went down to defeat when President Lyndon B. Johnson won in a genuine landslide.*

GOLDWATER-MILLER CAMPAIGN BUTTON. *This campaign button from 1964 depicts the conservative Republican alternative to the liberal Democratic ticket of Johnson and Humphrey.*

JOYCE CAROL OATES. *One of America's most prolific writers of fiction, Joyce Carol Oates was born in Lockport/ Millersport, and often sets her novels and stories in the western New York region. (Lockport Public Library files.)*

WYNDHAM LAWN HOME FOR CHILDREN. This former estate of Washington Hunt became the Home of the Friendless, and then the Wyndham Lawn Home for Children, after Hunt donated it to the community as part of his notable charitable works. The building still stands at the corner of Old Niagara Road and Lake Avenue in the town of Lockport, and continues to serve needy children. (Lockport Public Library files.)

MAIN STRET LOOKING WEST, 1922. This historic old postcard pictures a lively Main Street in the heart of downtown Lockport. (Lockport Public Library files.)

LOCKPORT PUBLIC LIBRARY. This contemporary photograph shows the East Avenue front entrance of the public library, home of the Local History Room where many of Lockport's historic records are stored and maintained.

NIAGARA COUNTY HISTORICAL SOCIETY. The headquarters of the Niagara County Historical Society, the Outwater Memorial Building, is located at 215 Niagara Street and features a museum and archives. (Brent Merrill photograph.)

ANCIENT ORDER OF HIBERNIANS MEMORIAL. This plaque and stone marker was erected on Main Street near the Big Bridge to honor the memory of the Irish immigrants who built the canal and contributed so much to Lockport's history. (Brent Merrill photograph.)

VETERANS MONUMENT. This memorial to Lockport's war veterans was designed by local artist Raphael Beck in 1930, and now serves as the centerpiece of Veterans Memorial Park (formerly the East Avenue Park) across the street from the Lockport Memorial Hospital. (Emily Riley photograph.)

LOCKPORT'S MAIN STREET, 1990s. These two photographs were part of a proposal for a historic renovation of Lockport's Main Street prepared by Mayor Thomas Sullivan's administration in 2003, indicating a need for some "sprucing up" if the vision for a revived tourism industry were to succeed.

VISTA FROM THE LOCKPORT LOCKS. This contemporary photograph taken from the lower level at the locks depicts the steeple of St. Mary's Church on Saxton Street and the "Big Bridge." (Brent Merrill photograph.)

ERIE CANAL DISCOVERY CENTER. Opened in the summer of 2005, the Erie Canal Discovery Center represents years of hard work on the part of a group of Lockport citizens with a vision, determined to preserve and honor Lockport's glorious past as the "Historic Jewel of the Erie Canal." The museum occupies the Hamilton House historic building across the street from the First Presbyterian Church on Church Street. (Emily Riley photograph.)

LOCKPORTIANS. This display in the Erie Canal Discovery Center and museum highlights the role of several prominent pioneering citizens such as Aunt Ednah Smith and Lyman Spalding who built the foundation of the town and city of Lockport, New York. (Emily Riley photograph.)

THE BECK MURAL. This historic painting by Lockport artist Raphael Beck, "The Opening of the Erie Canal, October 26, 1825" now graces the wall of the auditorium at Lockport High School. A replica forms the center display of the Erie Canal Discovery Center as well. (Emily Riley photograph.)

WELCOME SIGN. This sign, erected at the entrance to the city limits in a park at Transit Street and Lincoln Avenue in Lockport, focuses on Lockport as a community born of the Erie Canal, famous for its famous "flight of locks." (Emily Riley photograph.)

WELCOME TO HISTORIC LOCKPORT. This is one of several signs, posted at the city line at various locations in Lockport, in an effort to capitalize on Lockport's glorious past to welcome visitors and tourists. This sign, on East Avenue near the Lockport Town and Country Club, features the Kenan Center in addition to the locks. (Emily Riley photograph.)

COLD SPRINGS CEMETERY. This sign marks an entrance to one of Lockport's oldest cemeteries, located on an area between Chestnut Ridge and Cold Springs Road. In a sense, it is where part of the Lockport story begins and ends—the location of a wilderness outpost before the founding of Lockport, and the final resting place of Jesse Hawley. (Emily Riley photograph.)

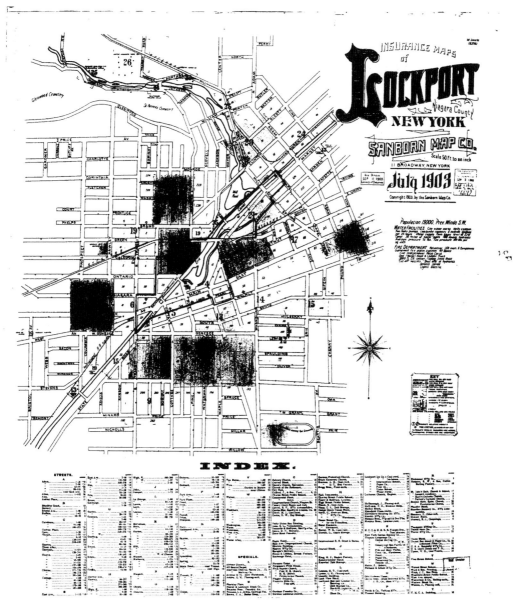

SANBORN INSURANCE MAP, 1903. This insurance map of Lockport depicts the city early in the twentieth century, indicating growth and structural improvements in terms of street layout and urban amenities like water facilities and a fire department. (Lockport Public Library.)

LIFE IN LOCKPORT. One of Lockport's first and best-known photographs, from the late nineteenth century, focuses on the famous flight of five locks. It captures the essence of the community as well: life on the canal in terms of transportation and surrounding manufacturing enterprises, the mules on the towpath, and the church steeple ascending from the bridge. (Niagara County Historical Society.)

Continued from page 64

> A political opposition to Masonry thus engendered, was gradually built up by those who were jealous of this increasing power of our Fraternity. In 1826, one man, lazy, intemperate, quarrelsome and dishonest, started a chain of events which, in due time, gave the political and religious enemies of Masonry their opportunity.

Morgan made arrangements with a Batavia printer and newspaper publisher, David Miller, to publish his account, with an eye towards making their fortunes, as they thought it would attract a wide audience. This partnership brought both of the men more trouble than they bargained for, for the Masons from several local towns sounded the alarm and were determined to stop them.

A campaign of propaganda to alert the brotherhood of Masons to the danger started with a short article printed in a Canandaigua newspaper on August 9, 1826: "Notice and Caution." Readers were told to be "on guard . . . if a man calling himself William Morgan should intrude himself upon the community." The local Masonic Hall had information on him, and encouraged their brethren to "observe, mark and govern themselves accordingly." Morgan was considered "a swindler and a dangerous man." The campaign had the desired effect, and led to efforts to intimidate Morgan and Miller. The Masons were willing to go to great lengths, and tried a variety of methods. The Ames Chapter of Lockport called a special meeting on August 11 and appointed a "Vigilance Committee."

The financial angle was the first one employed in Batavia and Canandaigua. Lawsuits for minor infractions were filed against both men—instigated by complaints from Masons—and subscriptions to Miller's newspaper were cancelled. A significant line was crossed into criminal activity when Miller's print shop was set on fire. Once crossed, the door to kidnapping and getting rid of Morgan permanently was opened. Even Clarence Lewis acknowledges that a good deal of organization went into the plan to silence Morgan—Masons from various places in western New York, including Canandaigua, Lewiston, Lockport, and Wilson met at Ganson's Tavern in LeRoy, resolved to "secure the manuscripts and, if necessary, to remove both Miller and Morgan from Batavia."

After Morgan was arrested for stealing a cravat and tie from a local tavern keeper, he was jailed in Canandaigua, released, and promptly re-arrested for an old debt of three dollars. These seemingly endless machinations failed to achieve the desired end, and Morgan was not successfully "removed" from Batavia at that time. On the night of September 12, however, the plot thickened. Several men came to the jail to pay the prisoner's fine, and convinced the wife of the jailor to release him into their custody. When she observed Morgan struggling with his captors, she shouted "Murder"—a cry that would have "tremendous consequences."

From this point, the story told by Lewis becomes difficult to follow, despite the copious details he provides. Suffice it to say that a carefully considered plan hatched by the Masons to transport Morgan from one town to another, changing carriages, drivers, and horses, picking up new conspirators at stops along the way and leaving others behind—all in the interest of deniability—swung into action. From Canandaigua, the relay proceeded through Rochester by way of the Ridge Road, then on to Lewiston and Wrights Corners, where the contingent of Niagara County Masons became involved. The end goal, apparently, was to take the prisoner to Fort Niagara and remove him from the country, settling him on a farm somewhere in Canada. Many tavern keepers along the way were involved in the scheme, as many of the stops and changeovers took place at their establishments.

The longest stop on the journey was made at Wrights Corners, and this is where the Lockport contingent took charge. The major players in this part of the drama included William Daniels, David Haigh, and Eli Bruce, the sheriff of Niagara County—now, apparently, breaking the law to serve the "higher end" of protecting the Masonic order and its secrets. Several of these men, after arriving in Youngstown, roused the ferryman from his sleep and crossed over into Canada. But their plans went awry, as the Canadians "were not ready to receive Morgan." He was returned to Fort Niagara and locked in the French powder magazine on September 14.

At this point things escalated—Morgan was crying out in fear of what was in store for him, while his captors, now armed, were determined to carry on with their plans. A call for help was relayed to Lewiston, where a new Masonic chapter was being installed. According to Lewis, "at least a dozen Lockport Masons were there," and a great many of the "Morgan conspirators." Several of these reinforcements proceeded to quiet Morgan with rum, and it was alleged that one of the principals said "if Morgan drank himself to death, so much the better."

Six men "delegated to make some disposal of Morgan so that he could not return to Batavia and go on with his Expose," led him out of the prison blindfolded. It was "a dramatic scene indeed, and one fraught with tragedy."

Morgan's fate from this point entered the realm of mystery, although numerous theories and rumors about his eventual disposition were offered in the following years. The goal was to "get rid of" Morgan, and leave no clues behind—whether that meant killing him, or simply sending him off to Canada, is the source of the greatest debate.

There is much conjecture about what really happened. The most thorough account of the affair, written by Lewis, states these facts: the whole series of events transpired over eight to nine days, from September 12 through 21, 1826, and that 69 Masons were successful in carrying out their roles. It was "the failure of the Canadian Masons to fulfill their part of the plot" that resulted in "catastrophe," and upset this "perfectly planned conspiracy." Lewis's record assumes a hyperbolic tone at this point, as he covers all of the possible scenarios offered to explain what really happened to Morgan. Among the highlights is the role allegedly played by Reverend Cuming, the same man who had delivered the stirring address at the laying of the capstone ceremony in Lockport the previous year. Charges against him were leveled by Thurlow Weed, leader of the Anti-Masonic party (and one "who hated Masonry intensely") formed in the aftermath of this episode, but denied by Cuming himself. Weed's purpose was to implicate a clergyman in the plot, while Lewis wished to suggest that the Anti-Masons circulated false charges and innuendo to uphold their side in the propaganda war that broke out after Morgan disappeared. The reverend was supposed to have offered this incendiary toast at the installation ceremony at Lewiston in the midst of the plot: "To the enemies of our Order, may they find a grave six feet deep, six feet long, and six feet due east and west."

Over the next few months and years, the rumor mill went wild. While the Masons "denied all charges of violence," and claimed that Morgan had been bought off by "$500 and a farm in Canada," the foes of Masonry claimed that he had been taken to the river in the dead of night, his body weighted down, and then "plunged into the dark and angry torrents of the Niagara." Speculations about Morgan's whereabouts, and even sightings of him—in Smyrna, Turkey; as a convert to "Mohammedism" living in Constantinople; or living the life of an Indian chief out west—proliferated. Attempts to discover his whereabouts were made, through newspaper notices and inquiries in various towns. Governor Clinton, well known as a Mason and "Grand High Priest in the order," issued a proclamation encouraging all citizens of New York to cooperate in the inquiry about "diverse outrages committed against the rights of persons in Batavia," and asked for the cooperation of Canadian authorities as well. There was a quite a storm brewing about the case, and Clinton was no doubt in a difficult spot as anti-Masonic sentiment escalated. In October, he offered a reward for information that might resolve the unanswered questions, and a specific reward of $300 for the "discovery of the offenders." Later that month, the first of several indictments was issued, and the subsequent trials would drag on for years.

David Miller capitalized on all the attention, and began to advertise for sale copies of William Morgan's *The Illustrations of Freemasonry*. So, it was clear that any plan of the Masons to prevent the publication of the book had failed. Miller hoped that all of the charges and counter-charges, especially those suggesting that Morgan had been murdered, would boost sales of the book. Later, in October of 1827, the case took a more dramatic turn when a body was washed ashore near Youngstown. Despite the fact that it was badly decomposed, the anti-Masonic forces insisted that it was proof that Morgan had been murdered, and his "widow" was enlisted to identify it. Eventually, to the disappointment of those determined to undermine the Masonic organization, it was determined that the body was actually that of a Timothy Munroe, who had drowned the previous month. To those in charge of encouraging conspiracy and counter-conspiracy theories, however, this did not prevent things from spiraling further out of control.

The most important result of the Morgan case for the nation—and the news spread well beyond the confines of New York—was the rise of the Anti-Masonic movement and political party. The first convention was held at LeRoy, New York in 1827, where the episode had started. Historians have interpreted this movement as a symptom of, or response to, the tidal waves of change—political, religious, social, and economic— sweeping across the country during the age of Jacksonian Democracy. The case in western New York convinced the opponents of Masonry that the organization was, in Tyler's words, "inconsistent with American liberties and with the responsibilities of citizenship." Those Masons who had enjoyed prominence were to be revealed as hypocrites who presented a threat to American values. To Whitney Cross, it was a "crusade, with marked affinity for most of the movements in religion and reform that would make western New York distinctive." The major issue was one of morality—the Masons had committed a crime, and demonstrated that their professed devotion to religious and democratic principles was a lie. Although the movement would soon disintegrate due its "centrifugal energies," its "impact may well have been the most comprehensive single force to strike the "infected district" during an entire generation—and Lockport was at the center of the action.

The ramifications in Lockport mirrored those on the larger scene. The plethora of propaganda produced in this struggle led to the founding of many newspapers (141 in the nation, 46 in the state of New York) including Lockport's *Niagara-Courier*. Churches and religious denominations turned against the Masons, and ministers hoping to retain their flocks were forced to resign their membership in the fraternal organization. The oath was deemed sacrilegious in many religious circles. In many communities, Masons were discriminated against and even persecuted. As Lewis wrote, this reversal of fortunes was stark in many communities, as Masons fell from the height of influence: "a Mason was hardly safe on the streets . . . his children were abused in school, and he was disfellowed from his church, said to be unfit for public office, and barred from sitting on juries (it was charged that the Masons tried to control the outcome of many conspirators' trials) . . . strangest of all, many women's organizations passed resolutions forbidding their daughters from marrying Masons!" In 1831, there was a convention of Anti-Masonic Republicans held at Lockport's Washington House.

The disposition of the numerous trials associated with the Morgan affair is the clearest indication of the extent of Lockport's involvement in this high-profile case. A grand jury was summoned in Niagara County in May of 1827 by Deputy Sheriff Hiram Hopkins, because Sheriff Eli Bruce was one of the leading conspirators charged. The sheriff packed the jury with Masons, and was exonerated. Bruce, David Haigh, Jared Darrow, and Orsamus Turner, publisher of Lockport's leading newspaper, were indicted for conspiracy in Canandaigua. Bruce was also summoned by Governor Clinton, and his lodge contributed money to his defense. But when he could not show the governor just cause why he should not be removed from the office of Niagara County sheriff, he was removed "forthwith." Lewis noted that Clinton's untimely death in February of 1828 "was a sad blow to Masonry, because his wise counsel might have averted some of the trouble that followed."

A trial for three Masons from the Lockport Lodge and Ames Chapter—Bruce, Turner, and Turner—was held in Canandaigua in August of 1828 (David Haigh had died). The charges were conspiracy and kidnapping, "to seize, carry off and hold" William Morgan. Numerous witnesses were called, including "Renouncers," who withdrew from Masonic membership and proved to be vociferous supporters of the anti-Masonic cause. In this and subsequent trials, the tactics employed by the accused and their supporters was to refuse to testify and answer questions and dissemble, making the case murky for the jurors. Bruce was found guilty because it could be proven that he had traveled in the carriage from Wright's Corners to Fort Niagara, but his sentence was suspended.

Lewis suggested that several "Masonic traitors," such as the deputy sheriff, had testified that Bruce issued instructions for a cell to be prepared for Morgan at the Niagara County jail. He was known thereafter as "Judas Hopkins."

Orsamus Turner repeatedly refused to testify, and several 30-day jail sentences followed. While he served his time, local supporters and friends visited him frequently, often bearing food and gifts. In March of 1831, Norman Sheppard and Dr. Henry Maxwell of Lockport were tried, but found not guilty.

The biggest "casualty" of justice meted out in Lockport was the sheriff, Eli Bruce, who eventually served a term of two years and four months. Because his incarceration had weakened his health, he fell "easy victim" and died during the cholera epidemic of 1832, a year and a day after he was released from prison. In loyal Masonic circles, he was referred to as "The Masonic Martyr," and admired for his steadfast refusal to testify against his friends and willingness to suffer financial hardship and incarceration. The lodge contributed financial support to his family as a show of their support.

Lewis makes a good statistical case for Lockport's important role in this national drama: of the 20 grand juries called, seven were in Lockport. Of the 15 trials, five were held in Lockport (second only to the seven held in Canandaigua). He also said that "the best legal talent in the country was engaged in defending the Masons." Judge William Marcy sat on the bench in one of the trials. Village residents John Jackson and William P. Daniels became famous as witnesses, "shrewd" at outwitting the prosecutors and judges; in fact, their evidence is quoted in various Morgan histories as "a masterpiece of evasive testimony." Such was Lockport's claim to fame in the opinion of Niagara County's long-serving historian, whose history of the Morgan affair was written with a bias in support of the Masons throughout.

Although Lockport Masonry suffered as a result of the anti-Masonic movement, for example, when anti-Masonic candidates won a majority of local votes in 1828, the damaging effects were not permanent. Across New York many lodges folded, but the Lockport chapters survived. For 10 years, from 1827 to 1838, the Lockport lodge "did not dare meet regularly." But when the hysteria subsided, the Masons regrouped; in fact, the *Souvenir Program Commemorating the Lockport Centennial*, issued in 1965, contained a full page ad, "Compliments of Masonic Fraternity and Concordant Bodies." Among the 14 organizations listed as having maintained their existence well into the twentieth century were the Lockport Lodge No. 73, the Ames Chapter No. 88, and the Bruce Council No. 15.

On the national scene the Anti-Masonic Party reached its apex in the presidential election of 1832, when William Wirt ran on that ticket as the first third-party presidential candidate in U.S. history. It quickly faded from view, however, as many anti-Masons joined the up-and-coming Whig party. During the remainder of the decade, attention began to shift away from the concerns of religious revival and reform in the burned over district, to the panic of 1837 and a series of international disputes that pitted the American republic against the British empire. In one of those cases, along the Canadian border, Lockport would be in the center spotlight once again.

The McLeod Excitement and the Patriot War

Anglo-American tensions escalated almost to the boiling point along the Canadian border in 1838, and were not completely resolved until 1842, when Secretary of State Daniel Webster was able to negotiate a treaty with Great Britain. The Webster-Ashburton treaty was a milestone in diplomatic history, as it settled all of the outstanding boundary disputes between the United States and Canada.

Along the way to this agreement, however, there was a good deal of saber rattling and occasional threats by Britain that these international incidents could lead to war. The "Aroostook War"—an undeclared conflict with no bloodshed—arose because of a boundary dispute between New Brunswick and Maine, and arguments over lumbering rights. President Van Buren sent General Winfield Scott to the troubled area after a U.S. land agent was seized by the Canadians, but a truce was arranged.

It was the "Caroline Affair" that would involve Lockport. The *Encyclopedia of American History* places this incident, called the "Patriot War" in most local accounts, in the context of simmering tensions aggravated by the financial panic of 1837, and an American sense of being insulted by several travel accounts—like Frances Trollope's—which presented the United States as a nation of "boors and blusterers." Violations of neutrality and disputed boundaries also came into play in the Niagara region.

The failure of an insurrection in upper Canada led its leader, a William Lyon Mackenzie, to seek refuge on an island in the Niagara River. American sympathizers with his plan to free part of Canada from the "yoke of British bondage" furnished him and his followers with provisions and arms, and they launched attacks on the Canadian frontier. At one point a Lockport resident, Major Benajah Mallory, was asked to take over the command of the "patriot forces." A loyal veteran of the Revolutionary War and the War of 1812, he refused, as the activity was not authorized by the U.S. government.

An American steamship, the *Caroline*, was used to transport supplies to the rebels, and on December 29, 1837, a band of Canadians crossed the river, burned the vessel, and sent it over the Falls. In the course of the melee, the Canadians killed Amos Durfee, an American citizen. Waves of patriotic indignation and Anglophobia swept over the United States, and President Van Buren warned American citizens to "desist from hostile acts" against Great Britain.

Tensions lessened, but three years later, a Canadian deputy sheriff named Alexander McLeod was arrested at Lewiston, New York for the murder of Durfee, after allegedly bragging about his role while in a bar on the American side of the border. He was confined in the jail at Lockport in 1841, and the town became a focal point in the dangerous international dispute.

Clarence Lewis wrote several articles about the "McLeod Excitement" and Lockport as a "hotbed." Even before the arrest of McLeod, Lockport residents were very interested in the Patriot War, and the community's first daily, the *Lockport Daily Bulletin*, was published to keep the town informed about the war's progress. With McLeod lodged in the Niagara County jail, and Britain demanding his release, a public meeting was called by citizens concerned about the security of the jail. Many surrounded it to prevent bondsmen from paying his bail and securing his release. Some accounts of the episode suggest that the people of Lockport rang bells and fired cannon to express their indignation, and demanded that he be brought to trial. Bands marched back and forth in front of the jail, playing the "Rogue's March" with "vigor." Lewis concluded his version of events by stating that after "diplomatic notes were exchanged between Washington and London," Secretary of State Webster sent the attorney general to Lockport and had McLeod secretly moved to the jail in Utica, lest preparations for war be carried too far. McLeod was released on a technicality, as the indictment had incorrectly referred to him as "Angus" rather than Alexander. Another version of McLeod's release, written by American historians Henry Steele Commager and Samuel Eliot Morrison, stated succinctly that "McLeod sober furnished an alibi for McLeod drunk." Tensions subsided, and Lockport's brief time in the international arena ended.

One last episode, shortly after the McLeod Excitement, is noteworthy of mention as a local matter attracting wider attention, with the Lockport jail again cast in a leading role. Clarence Lewis provided the details: two roommates who lodged together in Lockport engaged in a drunken brawl one night, and David Douglass shot and killed his friend. Found guilty, he was sentenced to death, and the first and only hanging in Niagara County history took place in the "corridor of the jail." There was a good deal of public sentiment against the hanging, and a story about the Reverend William Walton, pastor of the First Presbyterian Church, providing consolation to the condemned man was carried in the New York City papers, where poet John Greenleaf Whittier read it. He was inspired to write a tirade against capital punishment as a result, entitled "The Sacrifice," an example of small events in Lockport making the "big time" yet again.

Overall, these curious episodes from early nineteenth century history illustrate that Lockport continued to attract national attention, above and beyond its place in the national consciousness as the site of the famous flight of five locks. It was a far cry from the characterization of the lock city in the twentieth century as a "sleepy little town on the Erie Canal." Caught up in the tides of great change, Lockport contributed several stories to America's historical annals, providing an essential piece in some of the important puzzles of the age. Apart from the limelight, however, the town was also busy on the sidelines, steadily building on its foundations a more vibrant and prosperous community. Central to its future well-being and identity would be its churches and schools.

Chapter Six

A CHRISTIAN ENTERPRISE
OF VAST PROPORTIONS

*Do you know that there are at least thirteen denominational groups
functioning in the city of Lockport at the present time? That in our city of
approximately 25,000 population there are 25 church buildings?. . . That
this great religious and spiritual enterprise has been built up in about a
century and a quarter through the loyalty and oft-times extreme sacrifice of
thousands of folks? That the entire investment has been made in conserving
moral, social and spiritual values in the life of a growing community?. . .
The Christian enterprise in this city is one of vast proportions.*
—Reverend Harry A. Bergen, Pastor of the Plymouth
Congregational Church of Lockport, 1934

One noteworthy feature of Lockport's horizon, when viewed from the heart of
the canal that runs through the city, are the church steeples clearly visible to those
"sailing" through the locks. It was commented upon repeatedly by numerous visitors
during the nineteenth and twentieth centuries, and remains true today. Most of the
famous postcards and sketches of Lockport's locks are bracketed by the spires of St.
Mary's and St. Patrick's churches, and there is something especially fitting about the
prominence of St. Patrick's in the vista, as it was founded by the Irish immigrants who
built the canal.

In keeping with Tocqueville's observations about the pervasive influence of religion
in American life, many of the early histories of Lockport—like those of most other
communities—highlight the religious motivation and zeal of the early settlers. Despite
a multiplicity of different religious sects, they were all engaged in a common human
endeavor, as he saw it, of "harmonizing earth with heaven."

Orsamus Turner's *Pioneer History* noted that the "office of Christian ministers was
no sinecure upon the Holland Land Purchase," and that these brave and hearty souls,
after "itinerating," returned to their homes and labored with their hands, that they
might not be "chargeable upon the brethren." This early standard was in keeping
with that preferred by the Quakers who originally founded Lockport, and the later
arrival of those who practiced "priestcraft," and explains many of the early religious
tensions in the town. Turner praised the "faithful, disinterested, and devoted services"
of those who founded the first churches in the region, and encouraged the surviving
churches to "gather up their names, and cherish their memories," which all subsequent
commemorative histories have faithfully done.

Niagara County historian Clarence Lewis also wrote of Lockport's religious foundations during his tenure as the county's official historian. In one of his regular articles published in the Lockport *Union Sun & Journal* between 1952 and 1969, "Early Customs in Niagara County," he pointed out the "great spirit of cooperation that prevailed" across denominational lines most of the time, and the numerous missionaries and itinerant ministers who came to Lockport in the "rough pre-canal days" to lay the foundations of a civilized and respectable society. They continued their ministry during and after the building of the Erie, as the canal brought new life and sustenance to the community, and new social problems that required religion's healing powers.

At one and the same time, religion served as a source of contention and controversy as well as stability and cooperation. The key to understanding the genesis of Lockport's religious life can be found in the fact of geography and timing, for Lockport was created along the "psychic highway" of the Erie Canal at the time of the religious enthusiasm and revivals that took hold of western New York during the 1820s. In many respects it was an unbalanced time, a time of trying to strike the proper balance and maintain it over the next century, in the process of building a "Christian enterprise of vast proportions" that constituted the city in the twentieth century.

Religious Rivalries, Revivalism, and Millennial Inspirations

As so many religious and social historians have noted, Lockport is a microcosm of many of the movements that were spawned in the burned over district. Though it was not as famous as Rochester, which attracted national attention when evangelist Charles Grandison Finney preached to the multitudes in the "flour city" in 1831, Lockport felt the ripple effects of the "storm center" that was upstate New York. Denominational rivalries and cleavages defined the town's early days, and it was in the interplay of three groups—Quakers, Presbyterians, and Catholics—that the main drama of religious and social upheaval took place. Lockport serves as a good laboratory to observe many of the signs of strain that accompanied rapid growth in a competitive spiritual marketplace where religious groups struggled for position and a sense of security.

Whitney Cross's classic study reveals a region characterized by a lack of equilibrium, where religious, ethnic, and class tensions were interwoven into the fabric of community life. Change was the predominant force, whether looked at from the perspective of the "fires of the forest or those of the spirit." And the settlers, many of them from New England, brought a moral intensity with them to New York, part of their Yankee inheritance transplanted to new soil. Within two decades after the start of construction on the canal, Lockport could boast of a variety of churches representing multiple denominations: Baptists, Methodists, Presbyterians, Episcopalians, Lutherans, Congregationalists, and Catholics. And the number of churches established and built continued to grow steadily thereafter, due to both population increase and internal disputes that necessitated the establishment of another church by those who withdrew or were expelled from the original community.

This type of friction was all too common, both within and between denominations, and in the competition for souls among missionaries. Revivals brought both waves of religious enthusiasm to town, and campaigns ranged against the current "enemy:"

> The different campaigns made up a sectarian hierarchy. All Protestant churches united in condemning Catholics. All evangelical sects united, too, against Universalists and Unitarians . . . Baptists and Presbyterians cooperated in damning Methodists and freewill Baptists. Presbyterians all too often proved disagreeably intolerant of Baptists. To cap the climax, both Baptists and Presbyterians, particularly the latter, maintained a constant and bitter strife between the enthusiasts and the conservatives in their own denominations.

As Cross discovered, religious enthusiasm could spill over into dissent and tensions, and Lockport experienced some of this. But by and large, most of Lockport's schisms were mild compared with those of other canal towns—the pages of *Priestcraft Exposed* notwithstanding. When rivalry and controversy did arise, the local press and "radical journals" covered the strife, as much to sell newspapers as to keep the citizenry informed. As the history of Lockport's early years reveals, when difficulties arose within denominations, the leave-taking and forming of new churches was accomplished in relative peace.

The advent of religious revivalism was also explored in a more recent work of history by Paul Johnson: *A Shopkeeper's Millennium: Society and Revivals in Rochester, New York, 1815–1837.* Although Rochester is his focus, Johnson noted that revivals were strongest in manufacturing centers like Utica and Lockport as well as Rochester. He argued that "the crucial first generation of industrial conflict was often fought along religious lines," and that Finney's revival in 1831 helped to heal some of the divisions within the communities. The prominent business and religious leaders assumed responsibility for preserving law and order and promoting moral virtue, particularly when it came to keeping the "wild" side of life that accompanied the growth of the canal in check, and maintaining control of their manufacturing establishments. In the process, they enlisted in many social and religious causes such as abolitionism, temperance, and home missions—all part of the age's wider musings on the millennium.

At times, these social crusades and religious yearnings could appear to be working at cross purposes, as the missionary outreach of Protestants could fan the fires of nativism even as they tried to save the souls of the working class. Home Mission agencies could also produce bitter sectarian battles in the competition over which denomination was best suited to make over the religious landscape of western New York. Cross quotes Reverend William Wisner of Rochester, who would later serve as the pastor of Lockport's First Presbyterian Church for over three decades. He was said to have dreaded the thought that "while our missionaries are converting, their thousands of papal troops are coming over by the hundreds of thousands."

Many religious leaders were also influenced by Finney's new measures, which included the protracted meeting, the "village counterpart" of the rural camp meeting that flourished among Presbyterians. According to Cross, "It certainly played up the itinerant to the disadvantage of the settled minister, for it helped establish the notion that spiritual efforts under a person of particular talents would create a keener sense of spirituality than the ordinary course of events could achieve. Many would "echo the thoughts of a local clergyman, William F. Curry: by the by—before the millennium comes will not Christians hold 365-day-meetings every year? How many such meetings would it require to be held before the world should be converted?" These ministers and preachers held big dreams about the destiny of their "great state of New York," confident that if it were brought "over on the Lord's side," it might "turn the scale and convert the world."

One famous itinerant who visited Lockport in 1828 was Lorenzo Dow, a fine example of the propensity of the town to welcome the "peculiar" and the "eccentrics" that so many authors have commented on over the years. Dow was a famous Methodist preacher whose strange mannerisms, asthma, and zeal led him to be called "Crazy Dow." His theatrical, spell-binding style, characterized by a display of religious ecstasy made manifest in "jerking exercises," made him a favorite with the masses. Whatever craziness he exhibited could be exaggerated for effect, for he was a very effective evangelist. Religious historians have noted that his peculiarities and powerful preaching had a special appeal to the lower classes. He was an advocate, like most Methodists, of the downtrodden and neglected members of society. An early history of Niagara County, stating that "the youthful village seems not to have been overlooked by distinguished characters in their travels," reported that Dow made his appearance and "delivered one of his peculiar discourses in the woods in the rear of the Courthouse." He told a story of having reached out for souls on a packet boat as he made his way west in a most unusual manner. Near Medina, he "faked" that he was a barber, and proceeded to shave some of his fellow passengers before leaving in an "uncomfortable plight." One of the effects of Dow's visit to Lockport, according to this account, was to satisfy the desire of those who could not go abroad in search of curiosities.

These examples indicate that Lockport was caught up in the same waves of enthusiasm that affected other New York towns. An underlying hope of the people of this time and place, according to Historian Carol Sheriff, was that "in the face of their anxieties, the canal would fulfill the Republic's destiny to finish God's work—which would hasten the onset of the millennium." Religion provided a means of dealing with the changes caused by the coming of the canal, and as reformers and preachers worked to save the souls of their neighbors, they were also striving to improve the morality of their community. As Johnson said of Rochester, its leaders wanted to simultaneously "eliminate sin and pave the way for the Second Coming," confident that the future would bring economic and spiritual progress on earth as they awaited the onset of the millennium.

Lockport's First Churches

If it was difficult—if not impossible—to avoid some type of religious experience in western New York during the 1820s and 1830s, the same point could be made about encountering churches in the town's pioneer days. In Lockport, it was certainly true that the construction of houses of worship kept pace with the building of taverns and business establishments. In fact, a visible symbol of the tremendous changes taking place in the village that quickly supplanted the wilderness was the proliferation of churches.

According to a rule established by the Holland Land Company, the first group to erect a house of worship in the region was entitled to a grant of land, in the amount of 100 acres, for the support of a minister. But since the Quakers were the first to build their log meeting house in 1819, and they were opposed to this arrangement "as a matter of conscience" because of their objection to "priestcraft" and to paying ministers to preach, they refused the land. The Lockport Quakers could lay claim to a number of other firsts after buying their two acres for $24: the first school, the first wedding, and the first burial in the adjoining cemetery. They set the pattern for many later religious communities in terms of establishing their own school, burial ground, and social organizations in quick succession after building their churches.

And it was the Society of Friends that brought the antislavery sentiment to Lockport. Clarence Lewis wrote of a dramatic episode in Lockport's early days as part of his series of historical capsules, in a column entitled "Slavery Issue Engendered Bitter Feeling in the Village." He also wrote of the continuing influence of this religious body in another piece entitled "Quakers Ran Railroad to Aid Fugitive Slaves." Two slaveholders from Kentucky arrived in Lockport in 1823 to reclaim a fugitive slave. Pouncing upon Joseph Pickard, a barber, they were prevented from taking him away by several townsmen, and the case was handed over to the justice system. Joseph Comstock, "extensively known as a defender of the fugitive slaves" was aided by his brother Darius, who employed large numbers of Irishmen on his canal construction crew. During the hearing the prisoner jumped out of the window and was aided in his attempt to escape by a large number of canal laborers gathered outside. Although this plan failed, the judge declared him free "for want of proof," and "Friend Darius was heard to say that the prisoner could never be taken away from Lockport," proud of his community for standing up to unjust laws.

In 1834, the first recorded meeting of abolitionists in Lockport was held at the courthouse, led by Lyman Spalding and Moses Richardson, both well-respected citizens and Quakers. Since those early times, Lockport lore has focused on several possible sites that served as underground railroad stations, including a house on Summit Street and the YWCA building on the corner of Cottage and Walnut Streets. When Lewis wrote his articles, he made two very interesting observations: that Niagara County "as a whole was strong for abolition," and that there were "probably more free Negroes in Niagara County in 1853 than there were presently, a century later." It is clear that Lockport, because of its location near the Canadian border and its religious proclivities, participated in the larger "empire of benevolence" that developed in antebellum America. One of the main features of the revivalism associated with the Second Great Awakening was the call for those who became Christians, or had their faith renewed, to put that faith into practice, by performing good works. And both abolitionism and temperance caught hold of the people of Lockport.

After the Quakers refused the offer made by the Holland Land Company, the Presbyterians were only too happy to accept the plot of land on the Transit Road. They sold it and used the money to build a frame church on Court House Square in 1823. In terms of timing and prominence, the Presbyterians were set to become the movers and shakers of the Lockport religious community, and some of the resentment and differences inherent in their relationship with the Quakers can be gleaned from the pages of *Priestcraft Exposed.* As the Presbyterian denomination grew over time, some Quakers drifted away from the town of Lockport, making their way to the outlying communities of Gasport, Hartland, and Barker. In many respects then, the Society of Friends set the tone of early Lockport, but did not maintain a long term presence in the community.

Lockport's Presbyterian churches actually grew from the Lewiston Church, one of the "strongest of the thirteen churches in the Holland Purchase." Its history has been accessible because its official records have been preserved since the founding of the first Lockport church in 1823. In a pamphlet written by the church historian to commemorate "Our First One Hundred and Fifty Years," Gertrude Strauss notes that this was unusual for Lockport, as many of the official records of the community were destroyed by a fire in 1854.

The Reverend David Smith, minister of the Lewiston church, was probably drawn to Lockport because he was "concerned about the Godless condition of the community and resolved to remedy the situation." Apparently, the religious standards of the Irish immigrants in the village were not up to those of the Presbyterians, a fact noted by Strauss when she makes reference to "two different types of people" in Lockport. First were the "God-fearing Christian families of New England descent who came westward at the close of the 18th century . . . to settle here . . . innkeepers, lawyers, merchants, blacksmiths, jewelers, carpenters and masons . . . substantial men." The second group were the "workmen on the new canal . . . predominantly Irish, with some of German ancestry." They were a "motley crew—fighting, drinking and singing as they did the backbreaking work."

The Presbyterian community established in Lockport was comprised of 30 "God-fearing" members. A certificate filed in the county clerk's office notes that they resolved to call themselves "The First Presbyterian Society in the Village of Lockport." For the first two years itinerant preachers, visiting from the surrounding communities and from as far away as Huron, Ohio, took care of the church and its flock. In 1825, when the canal was finally completed, the first resident pastor, Reverend Aratus Kent, was appointed. The church membership grew under his care, and proceeded to set the moral tone for the village.

Strauss writes that "the church sternly upheld the moral and religious rules of the community. Its members came from all walks of life, with the strong guiding the weak." There was a good deal of reporting the sinful conduct of some members, followed by hearings before the session. The "guilty party" was given the chance to repent, and to "change his way of living." If the infractions continued, he could be publicly excommunicated and his name taken off the church membership. Such were the workings of the Presbyterian church in the canal town. The church fathers felt compelled to point out "any variation from virtuous living" and uphold the righteous standards of the Christian community, even if it meant casting out members of their own community. Behavior not condoned included "intoxication, petty thievery, scandal spread by gossip, unfaithful wives and husbands, and heresies." In the minutes of the session for 1835, it was noted that several younger members gave "no evidence of piety, to the great grief of their parents and the dishonor of religion," and their names were "erased" from the church rolls:

> Resolved—that children and youth being as able to live godly in Christ as persons of adult years, we cannot palliate, much less justify, the above persons, but deem them wicked and inexcusable, and in great danger of eternal ruin, unless they repent . . . our experience teaches us that children ought to be admitted to public profession of faith in Christ, with great caution and not until after they have, for some time, given evidence of Christian piety.

Though seemingly harsh in their judgments, the actions taken by the church fathers were not uncommon among early American evangelicals, especially in times of religious revivals or awakenings. And the possibility of repentance and rejoining the church, with guidance offered by the older and wiser members, was always available. The door to church membership was left open to those willing to repent and reform their lives.

Within the first few years of the founding of Lockport's First Presbyterian Society, several controversies that affected church membership arose in the village. The issue of the Sabbath was one that divided the Presbyterians from some of their fellow citizens, but also required discipline within the church. Strauss reported the case of one elder who met the stagecoach on Sundays and carried the mail to a local store used as a post office. This was considered sinful and a violation of the Sabbath, and he was "severely reprimanded," for the other elders did not believe that the mail must go through. Clearly, "keeping the Ten Commandments was more important."

As the membership grew, the need for a new church building became apparent, and in 1830 the original meeting house on Hawley Street was sold. A new brick church was built in 1831–1832 on the corner of Church and Ontario Streets, to accommodate a congregation that had grown to 355 members.

In 1838, however, the congregation split in an "orderly and constitutional manner." Forty members began to disagree with certain doctrines of Presbyterianism, and asked to be allowed to organize a new church in Lockport, "Congregational in its government and Calvinistic in doctrine." They respectfully requested "letters of dismissal and recommendation," and went on to establish the First Free Congregational Church of Lockport. A sign of the harmonious manner that prevailed in this split was the fact that the site chosen for the new church was on the corner of Church and Niagara Streets – next door to the Presbyterian Church.

Another reason for this parting of the ways within the original Presbyterian community was the anti-slavery cause. The Congregational Church denounced the institution of slavery, "refusing to receive as a member any person who justified it." The Presbyterians pursued a more hands-off policy regarding slavery, feeling that political issues should be kept out of church affairs. This difference of opinion was settled peacefully, and the issue of abolition and temperance would continue to be a concern for the religious citizens of Lockport.

The town's newspapers focused on these reform movements throughout the 1820s and 1830s. A notice about the first meeting of abolitionists held at the courthouse on July 21, 1834, reported that it was broken up by anti-abolitionists. Although there was a considerable anti-slavery sentiment present in Lockport, it was not unanimous, and the town would be divided along political and religious lines in the decades leading up to the civil war. On the local and humanitarian level, however, there was sufficient sympathy for the plight of a local former slave, one Gentleman George, who worked as a driver for the Tremont Hotel and wanted to buy the freedom of his mother and sister. The townspeople held a charitable fundraiser to help him achieve his goal. The Lockport Temperance Society was organized in 1830, led by a group of citizens that included Lyman Spalding and Joel McCollum, a rising businessman and civic leader who had migrated to Lockport in 1826 and would serve as first president of the Village Board. The meetings of the temperance society were held in a variety of churches, indicative of the ecumenical support for this cause in the young village.

As the Presbyterians prospered, they were led by one of their most beloved pastors, Reverend William C. Wisner, from 1842 to 1876. He had first served as pastor of the Second Presbyterian Church, which was formed in Lowertown as Lockport grew. In *Souvenir History of Niagara County*, published in 1902, the Reverends Robert Norton and Erastus W. Twitchell wrote of him in glowing terms as the man who rose in the "very midst of political furor"—the great conflict over slavery that "brooded above us like a storm cloud"—and "the crash of financial schemes." Economic difficulties almost wrecked the Second Presbyterian Church, and Wisner was called to the First Church, where his talents bloomed and he served as a unifying force:

> His infirmities were severe, and yet God's grace wrought triumphs through him, and thousands were won for Christ. His wisdom as a pastor was equaled only by his wisdom as a Presbyterial leader. . . . It was an era of controversies, and his co-presbyters always found him a safe leader . . . he lived to see and rejoice in the reunion of the divided forces of the Presbyterian Church.

His greatest achievement came in the form of the "remarkable" religious revivals of 1842 and 1843, which increased church membership dramatically—150 new members were welcomed on one Sabbath day. As his reputation as a preacher and theologian spread, Strauss noted that he was elected moderator of the General Assembly, which brought fame not only to Dr. Wisner, "but to First Church and Lockport as well."

On this firm and secure foundation built during Reverend Wisner's pastorate, the First Presbyterian Church continued to emerge as one of Lockport's leading religious congregations. A new meeting house or church was erected in 1855, and the chief source of income for this project, and the subsequent addition of a steeple in 1867—"the pride and joy" of the church because it could "be seen all over town"—was the pew rental system. The pews were auctioned off to the highest bidders, and many of Lockport's wealthiest citizens were Presbyterians.

The Commemorative 150th Anniversary booklet noted the importance of this status symbol: "one could tell upon entering the Sanctuary . . . just who the wealthier members were by their location in the room . . . these pews were jealously guarded by families for generations." In the later years of the nineteenth century, the First Presbyterian Church became actively involved in a variety of religious and social activities such as Sunday Schools, Home and Foreign Mission Societies, and Christian educational endeavors. Early in the twentieth century the practice of release time was promoted by the Lockport Council of Churches, which allowed public school children to be released from school on Wednesday afternoons and to go to their preferred churches, both Protestant and Catholic, for religious instruction. It was this spirit of cooperation across denominational lines that eventually won out over the rivalry and occasional animosity that periodically cropped up during the first decades of Lockport's history.

The Congregationalists, who branched off from the Presbyterians, underwent several other changes following the difference of opinion on abolition. According to Mr. and Mrs. Cleland Ward, who wrote the Congregationalist Church's centennial history in 1938, they believed in the "freedom of the church to inject her influence into every problem having to do with human welfare." Divided sentiments over slavery continued to be a source of tension in the town, engendering bitterness to the point where a Niagara County judge and pillar of Christ Episcopal Church in Lowertown, Washington Hunt, allegedly took part in the storming of a church that was hosting an anti-slavery meeting during the 1850s. The Congregationalists were also plagued by natural disasters. In 1852, while the congregation was singing the closing hymn at the First Free Church, a violent thunderstorm arose and a bolt of lightning struck and killed Deacon Crocker. Two years later, the Great Lockport Fire destroyed both the Congregationalist and Methodist Churches. Despite these setbacks, the Congregationalists of Lockport persisted and triumphed over adversity, establishing the East Avenue Church in 1890, and the Plymouth Congregational Church in 1920.

In addition to the Presbyterians and Congregationalists, other Protestant denominations that established a foothold in pioneer Lockport's religious landscape were the Baptists and the Methodists. In 1816, there were only five persons "entertaining Baptist sentiments" in Lockport and Cambria, but they organized a church and devoted themselves to the service of God, organizing the Niagara Baptist Association in 1823. Mary Shaw Parker's commemorative history written in 1928 starts off on a theme of trial and tribulation, noting the vicissitudes experienced by the "various little groups of our denomination." The original community was split and torn asunder on several occasions, but managed to persevere and lay the foundations for a healthy church in the town.

The Baptists advanced rapidly in Lockport until 1843, when "the evil days" befell them. Their "terrible calamity" stemmed from the followers of lay preacher William

Miller, who predicted the Second Coming of Christ in 1843. This movement encountered opposition and split religious communities, especially after Miller's expected millennium did not materialize on schedule. Lockport's pastor, Elon Galusha, accepted the Adventist teaching of Miller, and "the church was rent in twain." When the Reverend Galusha left over this matter, he took one third of the original Baptist community with him. The next pastor arrived in 1850, to a church "torn with dissension and full of misery." The name of the fellowship was changed to the Second Baptist Church in 1851, and changed back in 1861 to The Baptist Church of Lockport. Reverend Mason reorganized the church, and "harmony, peace and brotherly love prevailed." From 1872 to 1885, the community experienced a period of great revivals and emerged stronger than ever, taking up the work of the Baptist Aid Society and Sunday Schools, a fulfillment of the founders' original emphasis on the importance of providing for their children's religious education.

The Methodists came to Lockport thanks to the Reverend Daniel Shephardson, of the Ridgeway Circuit, who founded the Emmanuel Methodist Church in the early canal-building days. In "Emmanuel United Methodist Church, Celebrating 175 Years, 1823–1998," Elizabeth Herberger pointed out that of all the town's early denominations, the Methodists were the most itinerant in practice: Methodist ministers in the Genesee-Niagara region, like the Reverend Zachariah Paddock, "lived in saddlebags, not parsonages." But eventually a church was built in Lockport, on land deeded to the Methodists by Jared Comstock and his wife Susanne, who were Quakers.

The Reverend S. A. Morse, writing of his church in the 1902 *Niagara County History*, pointed out that "Methodism had to fight its way to the front in Niagara County . . . the "interdenominational comity" that had become a reality was "scarcely foreshadowed" then, as there were significant doctrinal disputes between the Methodists and the Calvinists, who considered their rival sects as little short of heretics. Once established in Lockport, however, the Methodists were pioneers in the temperance movement. Herberger reported that the First Methodist Episcopal Church took a pledge on October 10, 1829, voting to "abstain from the use of ardent spirits ourselves . . . we will not keep it in our houses except in cases of necessity . . . we will not furnish it to our laborers."

The element of social control was also evident in a joint decision by the Methodists and the Presbyterians to refuse to license a circus exhibition in the town. Opponents of the decision responded by coating the churches with tar. But the religious leaders refused to give in to such pressure: "this did not deter the church from taking a firm stand in matters where it believed the welfare and morals of the community were at stake." The slavery issue also proved vexing for the Methodists. In 1840, a vote to allow the church to host an anti-slavery meeting lost in a tie. Some of those opposed felt that these meetings became too raucous, and feared that church property might be damaged. For a brief period, the church split over the issue of slavery and abolition, but was reconciled in 1846.

By the time Reverend Bergen wrote of a "Christian enterprise of vast proportions" in 1934, many other churches had joined these early pioneering efforts, including

Episcopalians, Lutherans, Universalists, and the Salvation Army. It is clear that the early establishment of multiple Protestant churches in Lockport resulted in a pervasive "Christian" spirit, productive of both hostility and harmony, conflict and concord, at various moments in the town's early history. In the final analysis, the spirit of harmony triumphed, as differences were settled and the commonly held values of the community predominated. But a most complicating factor added to the religious composite was the presence and persistence of the Catholics.

The Catholic Minority Secures a Place in the Sun

The Catholic community of Lockport, like the city itself, was a product of the Erie Canal, for the first Catholics in the village were the Irish immigrant workers who came to dig the canal in 1821. Many were stonecutters and masons, whose skills were valued when it came to building the locks. Instead of following the work to the midwest when the canal craze caught on in Ohio and Michigan, many of them stayed on and settled permanently in Lockport. More Catholic immigrants arrived with the canal enlargement project of the 1830s and 1840s and the building of the railroad in the 1850s. They continued to arrive steadily thereafter, reflecting the migration patterns of European immigrants in search of employment in the United States throughout the nineteenth and twentieth centuries. Over time, these immigrants formed a thriving Catholic community in Lockport.

Historians of American Catholicism have written much about the parish as the foundation of the faith in the United States. Jay Dolan's study referred to the parish and its importance to the immigrants as the "hinge on which their religious world turned." In the early wilderness days, however, when the Irish were segregated on the outskirts of town, their religious needs were met by itinerant priests and those who visited from Rochester and other neighboring towns, like Father Patrick Duffy and Father Bernard O'Reilly. Father John Neumann, who went on to become the bishop of Philadelphia and was later canonized a saint, was assigned to the mission territory of western New York at the beginning of his career. Eventually, the priests were invited to celebrate mass in the courthouse, until the local Catholics could organize their own parish and build a church. These regular gatherings of the Irish immigrants in Lockport were among the first to take place in the region that would become the Catholic Diocese of Buffalo.

St. John's Church in Lockport, built in 1834, is generally considered to be the first parish building constructed in the Buffalo Diocese. The land was donated, in a pattern often repeated in Lockport's religious history, by men outside the religious community; in this case, the land was given to the Irish by two of the town's leading citizens, Joel McCollum and Edward Bissell. Lyman Spalding, becoming something of a philanthropist as well as a businessman, donated another lot, which was sold to raise money for the construction costs. Although he took issue with the Presbyterian "priests" who sought to impose their standards on the town, he was generous enough to help the Catholics establish their first church.

The cornerstone of the parish, named after and dedicated to St. John the Baptist, was laid in August of 1834 on Chestnut Street, on the corner of what would become McCollum Street. Much of the work was done by the parishioners themselves, when they were not engaged in working on the canal or in the stone quarries. The walls were up and the roof under construction by the end of that year, allowing the Catholics to celebrate mass in their own church on Christmas. The building was formally blessed by Bishop Dubois.

The first pastor was Father Mangan, who came for two or three weeks at a time and encouraged the people in their efforts to finish the church building. The Reverend Patrick Costello, who had visited regularly from his home church in Greece since 1836, was assigned to reside in Lockport in 1839. He took charge of St. John's Parish, while also remaining responsible for the mission territory of Niagara and Orleans Counties. A succession of priests followed, many of them of Irish heritage. A rectory was built after the church was finished, so that the pastors no longer had to board with families in private houses in town.

The first surviving parish records of St John's are those of Father McMullen, who served from 1842 to 1850. The parish was growing, and the church acquired a plot of land that became the town's first Catholic cemetery. Under the leadership of Father Thomas McEvoy, a total abstinence society was formed and a school was set up in the church basement. The Diocese of Buffalo was formally established in 1847, and the first bishop, John Timon, paid a visit to St. John's in Lockport. Elaborate preparations were made by the members of the parish, who constructed an ornate archway to welcome their bishop. Bishop Timon confirmed 175 people during his visit to the parish.

During the pastorate of Father Michael Creedon, a demonstration of greater Lockport's ambivalence toward the Catholics in their community took place, indicative of the national phenomenon of nativism and anti-Catholicism. As described in "A Centennial Souvenir of St. John the Baptist Church, 1827–1934," rumors accusing the local Catholics of storing arms in the basement of the church circulated on the streets of the town in 1856, at the height of the Know-Nothing political party's prominence. Father Creedon decided that the best course of action was to meet the hysteria head on. He conducted a tour of St. John's, revealing that there were no arms or any evidence of a papist plot against the Protestants, and "they left indignant that people should be duped by such a slander." Other examples of the relatively peaceful relations enjoyed by the Catholics and Protestants of Lockport had appeared in the secular and religious press. At the time of the Protestant Crusade during the 1830s, the *Niagara Democrat* published a notice about *The Awful Disclosures of Maria Monk*, the chief anti-Catholic tract of the era. It was described as "promoting a shameless combination of bigotry and avarice." On January 19, 1856, the Diocesan *Buffalo Catholic Sentinel* published a short piece on the conflicting opinions about Catholics in Lockport, which ended on a positive note. *The Daily Journal* had "nobly stepped forth in defense of the Catholic people from the bigoted attacks of the *Lockport Courier*," which had advertised a new edition of the *Maria Monk* book. Readers were warned against the "dirty pamphlet," and reminded that the editor of the *Courier* had blackened its reputation, and in the face of proof of the falseness of the charges, "was obliged to conceal his bile until he could vomit it in the Know-Nothing Lodge."

A Reverend W. F. Curry, Protestant minister in Geneva "known and respected by the citizens of Lockport," had investigated and written of his dismay at the revival of anti-Catholicism: "I am sorry this miserable thing is revived . . . there will be no difficulty in presenting a mass of evidence of its utter falsehood." He proceeded to speak of his own experience in Montreal, the site of many of Monk's charges about her experience in the nunnery, and concluded that her book was one of the "most impudent impostures that was ever put forth by an abandoned woman. . . . If the opponents of Popery can do no better than to raise this ghost, they must be hard pressed indeed, and sore afraid." This testimonial speaks loudly of the generally hospitable reception enjoyed by the Catholic minority in Lockport, and their subsequent ability to prosper and grow as a religious community.

Under Father Creedon's term as pastor, it became apparent that the congregation had outgrown the church building, and he purchased two lots on the corner of Church and Caledonia Streets. After he was transferred to Auburn, New York, Father Bede took over the building project. The cornerstone for this new church was laid in 1857, and it was completed and dedicated in 1863, with the Reverend William Gleeson as Pastor.

The year 1863 was an auspicious one for the Catholics in Lockport for another reason, as Father Gleeson had the foresight and wisdom to send to Belguim for a religious order of nuns to staff the Catholic schools. At first they were met with some suspicion by the non-Catholics, proof that some elements of nativism persisted in Lockport. Subject to occasional insults, they didn't wear their habits, as they knew this attracted unwanted attention. According to the St. Patrick's Parish History, published in 1989 to commemorate its 125th anniversary, "time brought relief" and the townspeople realized that the sisters were not "foreign agents." The Sisters of St. Mary of Namur have faithfully served the community since that time, and continue to teach in Lockport's Catholic school system today. They have educated generations of students at the various parish schools, St. Joseph's Academy for women, and DeSales Catholic School.

When the new church was completed, the old building on Chestnut Street became a school conducted by the sisters. But the Catholic population of Lockport continued to grow, especially in Lowertown, and it became necessary to reopen the old church and reconstruct the parish of St. John's there. The newer building on Church Street was transformed into St. Patrick's Parish—especially fitting for the Irish population—a decade after it had been dedicated as the Church of St. John the Baptist. St. Patrick's soon became one of the most impressive religious structures in the community, built of the native stone harvested from the local quarries by immigrant masons. In 1869, Father Patrick Cannon was appointed pastor of St. Patrick's, where he served for 53 years, "guiding the parish with unusual fervor and devotion." Clarence Lewis noted that at the time of his death in 1922, his dedicated years of consecrated service made him the "dean of Lockport clergymen," beloved by Catholics and Protestants alike. He supported a strong spiritual life in the church, and his surviving record book is filled with notices of regular parish missions, conducted by Jesuit, Passionist, Dominican, and Redemptorist orders. Historian Jay Dolan's study of *Catholic Revivalism* makes reference to a "miracle cure" of a paralytic woman that occurred at one of these parish missions in Lockport in 1876. Father Cannon was also a true "brick and mortar" pastor, dedicated to creating a church building to outshine the Protestants. Under his leadership the church was expanded and the tower and the two smaller turrets were built. The local newspaper wrote of the completion of the tower of St. Patrick's and the "dramatic raising of the stone cross at the top of the spire . . . this capped the climax of all the church steeples in the town, inasmuch as it is the only one built entirely of stone of which the Lock City can boast." He was also responsible for expanding the cemetery and building the new school and the Sisters of St. Mary Motherhouse and convent school, St. Joseph's Academy, adjacent to the church.

In addition to the first parishes of St. John's and St. Patrick's, the Catholics of Lockport established three other churches, all national parishes associated with specific ethnic groups. The German Catholic community was formed into a separate religious body by Bishop Timon, and organized into St. Mary's Parish in 1859. They took over a church building on the corner of Buffalo and Saxton Streets, formerly owned by the Episcopalians, and built their own church on the same spot in 1885. In the twentieth century, an influx of Italian immigrants came to settle in Lockport, and they established two separate parishes in keeping with their old-country regional loyalties: St. Joseph's Parish on Market Street in the heart of Lowertown (1912), which served the immigrants from Sicily and southern Italy; and St. Anthony's Parish in the west end (1929), whose communicants came from northern Italy.

Over the course of a century, then, the Catholics of Lockport successfully secured a place in Lockport's religious landscape and earned the respect of their fellow citizens. As the centennial history of St. John the Baptist Church pointed out, Catholics deserved to be recognized along with the first pioneers, for "the growth and progress of the city from the beginning have been bound up with the growth and progress of Catholicity." In 1987, the local William J. Ryan chapter of the Ancient Order of Hibernians, an Irish Catholic fraternal organization, in conjunction with the New York State Irish Legislators, underscored this fact by erecting a stone monument on the big bridge near the canal locks. It offers something of a resolution of the ambivalent sentiments often expressed toward the Catholics in their adopted home in the early days, with a simple inscription: "In memory of the many Irish immigrant laborers whose endurance in the construction of the Grand Erie Canal brought untold wealth to the area in which they settled." It also serves as a reminder of the power of history to restore a sense of balance to the past, especially after the somewhat turbulent religious days of Lockport's founding, when "unbalanced times" seemed an apt characterization of western New York.

From Religious to Educational Foundations: The Union School System

The historical annals of many American towns often focus on the twin pillars of church and school as indicative of the community's values and spirit, and Lockport is no exception. The earliest schools in Lockport grew out of the religious establishments, with the first classrooms often located in church buildings, whether Presbyterian, Methodist, or Catholic. The first school was taught by Miss Pamela Aldrich in the Friends Meeting House. Soon thereafter, better accommodations were provided by a Mr. Wilson, who built a log building at his own expense on Main Street that would serve as a school. It was a combination of public and private enterprise, as he received a stipulated sum for each pupil. Rooms above stores and in town halls also served as schoolrooms. In 1824, the Masonic lodge even proposed the idea of establishing its meeting hall in the upper story of a building that would serve as a school, but this idea was deemed "inexpedient." In 1832, according to a timeline compiled by Lockport Attorney Anthony Lewis as part of a public address on the "Old Schools of Lockport," the Exchange Coffee House became a school.

At this time when the boundaries between secular and religious education were being drawn, many of the Catholics persisted in sending their children to separate parochial schools, fearful that their children might lose the faith in the public school system, and the parochial school system of Lockport endures to this day at DeSales, the former high school that now serves as a consolidated grammar school.

Lockport's greatest claim to educational fame, however, stems from the fact that it gave birth to the Union School system in 1847, believed to be the first public high school in the United States. A consolidated structure comprised of both primary and secondary education, it was certainly the first such system in New York, and served as a model for many other school districts. Prior to this innovation, Lockport's educational enterprise was composed of both district and private schools. The Lockport Classical School of the 1830s and 1840s was an example of private education—the students all paid tuition to attend—with a dose of religious influence added in when the Reverend Windsor of the Episcopal Church served as a teacher.

The Union School, the real foundation of the public school system in Lockport, was the brainchild of Sullivan Caverno. A graduate of Dartmouth College, Caverno had served with distinction as the principal of the Lewiston Academy, and wanted to improve the quality of education in Lockport, making it an exemplar for the state. Some citizens of Lockport had complained that they had to send their children away for a quality educational experience, and Caverno resolved to remedy this state of affairs.

He devised a plan, according to historian Clarence Lewis, that "embodied the idea of a school system that would not only embrace the common schools, but schools or departments that would offer high school training as well." He submitted his plan to prominent national educators for their advice and insight, including Horace Mann of Massachusetts, and Professor Sanborn of Dartmouth.

The first Lockport Union School opened in 1848 near the New York Railroad Depot, and was designed to serve the needs of all students on the basis of equality, rich and poor alike, supported by a system of public taxation. The initial reaction to the idea of public support and the extent of the expense was one of opposition. Chroniclers of early Lockport history refer to the threat of "mob violence" over the issue. But the opposition was overcome, and Caverno, with the help of members of the assembly and the senate, introduced a bill into the New York state legislature that became law. It authorized the creation of the Board of Education of the Village of Lockport, with a board of trustees, and consolidated the existing seven school districts into a common union district. Among the trustees who initially served were Caverno, Hiram Gardner, and Lyman Spalding.

Provisions were also made for support of a public library through the school's tax system. The first library was established on the third floor of DeLong's shoe store. A separate school for the African American children was also set up. Clarence Lewis reported that the cornerstone of the second Lockport Union School building was laid in 1890 with "full Masonic ceremonies"—the way Lockport had grown accustomed to marking all of its great moments. During the twentieth century, many new school buildings were constructed to accommodate the city's growing population. These were generally named to commemorate the memory of prominent citizens and educators, such as De Witt Clinton Elementary School in 1925, and John Pound and Washington Hunt in 1930. To celebrate the 100th anniversary of the founding of the Union School in 1948, the town produced a chorale play entitled "Through Alma Mater's Halls." A copy of the script, preserved in the Public Library's Local History Room, sings of Lockport's pride "in the fundamental values of free education and its importance to the state . . . coming generations will realize full well the noble step we have taken" and "the great asset that it will be to the mentality and posterity of the community."

Despite the grandiloquent style of the writing, and the hometown booster tone it adopted, the section on the "Union School of Lockport" in the 1878 *History of Niagara County* sheds additional light on the importance placed on the schools in Lockport's community life and history, alongside its pride in its religious foundations:

> The Union School has been justly called the pride of Lockport. Nature has done much to give to Lockport advantages possessed by few other places; the State of New York built the Erie Canal . . . the county of Niagara made it her shire town and business center, and the market place for the abundant, rich and varied products of her fertile soil . . . Lockport as a municipal corporation can claim no credit for these advantages and developments. But she may rightfully claim a credit for that which has given her an enviable reputation and rank among the cities of the state. Her Union School system has given her such character, and contributed, in large part, to her material prosperity.

This theme is echoed, in a more objective fashion, by Carol Sheriff as she tied the town's religious, educational, and business life together. For many communities created as a result of the Erie Canal, time would demonstrate that it was "not necessary to choose between material progress and a godly society." The lucky communities could have it all, and Lockport had its fair share of good fortune.

Chapter Seven

THE POWER OF WATER CREATES A CENTER OF PROGRESS

Particular effort has been made to mention the pioneer business men, professionals, leaders in industry and inventors, who made this place the theatre of their achievements. They builded wisely and well, and laid deep the foundations of present prosperity. The public benefit was ever their aim. . . . Some of their descendents are still with us, and pursuing the paths their fathers trod, with knowledge and means which their progenitors largely lacked, helping to extend and beautify their inheritance. Many others are scattered over the broad face of the world, and seldom is found one whose heart does not warm at the mention of their former residence. Old Home Week will probably bring many of these wanderers to revisit former scenes, and their welcome will be sincere and cordial.
—Joshua Wilber, *Lockport Old Home Week Souvenir*, 1910

From the beginning, Lockport's economic health and community well-being was dependent upon water, for it was the water of the canal that gave life and continued sustenance to the town and city. Once established, the key to its future progress and prosperity was to be found in harnessing and controlling the surplus water supply of the canal, giving rise to Lockport's reputation in the decades following the opening of the canal and into the twentieth century as the "City of Smokeless Power."

In addition to the preeminent force of water power, two other factors set the stage for Lockport's future growth: its location and transportation systems. While the canal was under construction, the major businesses of the village catered to the needs of the incoming settlers and travelers. Lumber, saw and grist mills, and taverns and hotels were paramount. Once Lockport was permanently fixed on the map, this pattern continued. In addition, it became known for its agricultural products—part of the rich fruit belt that extended across the towns of Niagara County—and as a center for the manufacture and shipping of flour, as described in a commemorative booklet from 1925: "The fruits of the orchards and the grain of the farms that surround her boundaries rank first in quality markets and give evidence that here is a land of promise, a garden of fulfillment."

A logical outgrowth of its geographic location and the natural resources of the escarpment was a thriving stone quarry business. The limestone from this region was in high demand throughout New York and beyond.

As its economic fortunes flourished, the social and civic life of the community blossomed. The tradition of Old Home Week in Lockport, a time to celebrate the city's progress and ingenuity and recall its proud heritage and famous citizens, was celebrated at regular intervals in the twentieth century. The commemorative publications marking these occasions shared a common celebratory tone. From the observations of Joshua Wilber—Lockport's "venerable druggist" and amateur historian—in 1910, through the Historic Souvenir Booklets of 1925 and 1935, the confidence and pride of the community was clearly evident. Attention was focused on the Erie Canal as the "progenitor" of Lockport and an incentive to expansion: "Lockport grew into power and prominence beyond even the expectations of her first pioneers. Hotels and taverns began to expand. . . . Everywhere there existed an air of permanence, growth and prosperity."

In the 1925 centennial booklet, a section on "The Beginning of Giant Enterprise" related the surplus water of the canal to the overall vitality of the town after 1825: "Manufacturing enterprises began to spring up, schools broadened their scope, churches increased their congregations, and merchants enlarged their stores." Clearly, the life-giving "spring" of water that ran through the center of the town was a major determinant of its fate.

The Contest for Water Rights

Securing the rights to the canal's surplus water produced a controversy involving Lockport's most ubiquitous pioneering citizen, Lyman Spalding, beginning with the opening of the Erie Canal. It was a controversy that went on for years, exacerbated at times by the canal enlargement projects, and it would come to involve numerous businessmen, investors, politicians, and the state of New York.

In Lockport's many anecdotal histories, the story of the struggle for control of the rights to the water produced by the canal looms large. Although many of the versions of this story are partisan, all of the accounts agree that the surplus water was the key to Lockport's growth as a manufacturing city with diversified industries. Much of Lockport folklore focuses on the advent and successive waves of new forms of power over time—from the physical power of the Irishmen who first built the canal, through the power of the surplus water, and later versions of steam and hydroelectric power. It is the constant thread woven through the fabric of the story of the growth of a healthy economy in the village and city of Lockport, from the mid-nineteenth century through the opening decades of the twentieth century.

One very informative account is found in Alexis Muller's commemorative booklet on the 150th anniversary of the Erie Canal, *Looking Back so that we move ahead*. It is obvious that the author has an agenda here, when he writes of a little "morality play" and the political overtones of the conflict, referring to the greed and power-hungry mentality of "the Establishment:" "chalk up another in Lockport's long list of penny-pinching mistakes." But he offers a more objective assessment in his chapter on "the power story," tied in with the town's growing pains:

State officials arranged to sell the rights to use such surplus water wherever it was available along the canal. This would produce revenue which would help pay for the canal and would provide new sources of power to build up industries.

The story of this hydraulic power here in Lockport began, continued and ended in controversy. The beginning and ending, although 110 years apart, show remarkable similarity . . . there were legal owners of the water rights . . . there were other parties who wanted to virtually steal those rights . . . there were public hearings, petitions, legal maneuvering and years of uncertainty. And in both cases the people of Lockport were the eventual losers.

The tale began in 1825, when the state of New York leased the right to use the surplus water of the canal in Lockport, as it passed from the upper to the lower level, to the partnership of Richard Kennedy and Junius A. Hatch. Lyman Spalding, rising entrepreneur, had purchased land from Darius Comstock and resolved to build a flour mill. He assumed that he had the right to make use of the water, essential power for the mill, because it ran across the land he owned. But his assumption was wrong, and he was embroiled in trouble and litigation thereafter, as his finances rose and fell with the water supply. Spalding, the state, and the men who leased the water rights all appreciated the power and potential for profit that it represented. Despite Spalding's standing in the community—owner of the largest saw mill in town, proprietor of the American Hotel, real estate developer, newspaper editor and publisher, philanthropist, president of the Village Board (1830), treasurer of Niagara County, postmaster (1860s)—he experienced the vicissitudes of fortune associated with the politics of water rights, seeming powerless at times to maintain the value of his investments. He would suffer losses, sell out, and return to a new venture later—coming back from adversity to success on a veritable roller coaster ride.

Carol Sheriff's focus on Spalding as Lockport's renaissance man in her book *The Erie Canal and the Paradox of Progress* illustrates the that "the economic mobility accompanying the market revolution worked in two directions—up and down." Spalding interjected moral overtones into these battles over water rights, suggesting that the state and the Canal Commission had a responsibility to assist businesses essential to a town's economy, particularly when that business—like his flour mill—was a major employer.

Spalding's assumption about his right to use the water was understandable, as he agreed to assume Comstock's bid when he bought the land. Although Kennedy and Hatch owned no land on which to make use of the water, they made the highest bid of $200 rent annually, and were awarded the rights. Spalding went ahead with his plan to build a sawmill and a grist mill in the basin of the locks, recalling in his diary: "as the water was turned on my land, [I] proposed to use it, believing the Commissioners would not allow the water to be shut off and run through the locks, as this would interrupt navigation and incommode boats running on the canal."

He proceeded to build a massive structure, several stories high, which became the center of the town's incipient industry and became the first enterprise to harness the canal's water power in Niagara County. Spalding recalled this episode as a bitter learning experience, an education in what Muller's account characterized as a scarcity of ethics in business and political life: "I made a great mistake in supposing our Canal Commissioners to be honest and not subject to be bought up." He also regretted not buying Kennedy's interest, offered to him for $300 after the man died; it would have saved him years of litigation and grief.

Once the mill was up and running, it became a profitable enterprise. But things became "very tense in 1827–1828," as Clarence Lewis relates in his accounts. Spalding had been confirmed in his right to use the water on his land, without interference, until the political plot thickened.

A group of capitalists from Albany, the state capitol, bought up all the land below the escarpment, hoping to turn this into Lockport's industrial center "that could surpass the Upper Village in every way"—the beginning of the rivalry between lower Lockport and the already established upper section of town. They had purchased Hatch's water rights, realizing that this was essential to making their investment pay off and establishing the supremacy of what would become known as Lower Town. As Clarence Lewis stated, "only Lyman Spalding stood in the way of this grandiose plan of the Albany Land Company."

The situation escalated when the Albany speculators proceeded to dig a ditch through Spalding's land, by-passing his mills and robbing him of the surplus water. "Mr. Spalding's friends rallied to his support and drove the workmen away." Some accounts note the potential of the confrontation for spilling over into violence. The land company, however, had the power of the canal commissioners behind it, particularly Samuel Young, Henry Seymour, and W. C. Bouck. And they had an on-site agent to represent their interests in Lot Clark, who established a law office in Lockport.

Seymour was accused of profiteering and using his influence with the legislature to circumvent the law, having himself appointed to supervise the western section of the canal near Lockport. Spalding's account accused these men of trying to set up an "opposition town or rival city," and damaging not only his personal business but the welfare of the entire upper village. In Sheriff's interpretation, he "linked his personal fortune—estimating the mill's value in 1830 at $60,000—to that of the greater good." His financial ruin would have ripple effects, not only on the workers who would lose their jobs, but on farmers from the surrounding area who relied upon his mill.

The case moved into the court system, where it produced "hundreds of pages of argument, petitions, demands, replies and decisions," according to Muller's telling of the tale, sympathetic to Spalding as the lone man fighting against the establishment's dastardly tactics of "nepotism, favoritism and outright theft." Judge Marcy urged a compromise as the only solution, but he was ignored. Eventually, the bad publicity led Commissioner Seymour to resign, and Spalding to sell out:

> After much litigation and annoyance attended with expense and absence
> from my family, I thought best to sell the mill property on the easterly side

of the basin . . . bought 300 feet along the basin with the water from the first run of the Spalding Mill, and commenced in 1833 building the overshot saw mill.

So, although Spalding may have been down after this first battle over water rights, he didn't remain out for long, buying back some land with legal title to a portion of the original surplus water. His rise to prosperity and local fame continued—though not without further forks in the road.

Like the town, Spalding expanded his business interests. In "Pioneer's Interests Varied: Silkworms to Sawmills, Publications to Magazines," county historian Lewis described his ventures into the coal business and an unsuccessful venture into the cultivation of silkworms. He was a risk-taker throughout his life, always giving back to his adopted community in some fashion or another. In 1841, one of Lockport's multiple fires destroyed his milling business and he lost over $100,000. By 1842, he rallied, noting in his diary: "Commenced my own work again—after passing through the fiery ordeal of Bankruptcy." Sheriff describes him as a man of "remarkable faith in upward mobility, and continued prosperity"—as if the fires he passed through, both literally and figuratively, made him more determined to persevere and move in new directions. Clarence Lewis summed up Spalding's central place in Lockport history in these words: "He was destined to become one of our leading citizens and to engage in such a diversity of business and cultural activities as to make a person, even of this hectic age [1952], wonder how he survived until 1885."

The development of Lockport's surplus water power remained an essential part of the town's industrial development, eventually leading to the creation of a multiplicity of manufacturing enterprises. In 1856, the Hydraulic Raceway/Hydraulic Power Company was organized by William Marcy and Washington Hunt, after buying the Albany Land Company. Once again Lockport's movers and shakers were behind this new company, illustrating the fact that a network of political and business connections helped explain a man's opportunities and increased his chances of success in a small town.

Hunt had made his way into Lockport society since arriving in 1828. He served as a law clerk for Lot Clark, and rose steadily up the political ladder, serving as a judge and becoming the governor of New York—the only resident of Niagara County to serve in that office—in 1850. Marcy was also a former judge and governor, well-connected across New York. The hydraulic raceway, the tunnel that conveyed water, would be the main power source for the next stage of Lockport's industrial development, coinciding with the town's rising prosperity. Hunt and Marcy's company enlarged the raceway running along the bank of the canal behind Main and Market Streets, which made the expansion and diversification of Lockport's manufacturing base possible, and the growing city also acquired rights to the water for public use in 1864. The Erie, of course, remained the heart and soul of the village and its major source of prosperity—and there were changes ahead for Lockport's grand canal.

The Enlargement of the Canal and the Coming of the Railroad

A decade after the opening of the Erie Canal, it had proven to be such an unparalleled success for both New York and the nation that the state legislature authorized the first of several enlargement projects in 1835. The plan called for constructing double sets of locks at various locations, and expanding the canal to a width of 70 feet and a depth of 7 feet. Travel was so heavy on the canal that complaints about nuisances and its limitations—backed up boats and bottlenecks, insufficient width to accommodate the heavy traffic, "low bridges," and needed repairs on both bridges and aqueducts— swelled. Carol Sheriff summarized the problem well: "the dramatic success of the canal combined with its modest dimensions to create vastly overcrowded conditions." If the progress associated with the canal was to continue, it would have to be expanded and updated. One of the most respected voices in favor of the improvements was Jesse Hawley, who had settled in Lockport. In 1840, he petitioned the legislature, asking that the timetable be speeded up, and that pleas to cut costs by reducing the dimensions of the enlargement be ignored. Once again, the essay he wrote was a testimony to his enduring eloquence in sustaining the reality of what had once been his dream:

> No single act—no public measure—except the Declaration of Independence, and the formation of the United States Constitution, has done so much to promote the public prosperity, and produce a new era in the history of the country, as the construction of the Erie Canal.

Hawley died in 1842, before this phase of the enlargement was finished. Soon after the construction project commenced, it was complicated by politics and economic difficulties, and would not be completed until 1862. By then, it was once again too crowded, and the state embarked on a seemingly endless cycle of expansion and improvements into the twentieth century. In one of his columns on Lockport's past entitled "First Canal Enlargement Plagued by Petty Politics" (1967), Clarence Lewis reported that Lockport's piece of the project started in 1838. It was an economic shot in the arm for the town, employing 800 men and keeping Lockport's limestone quarries busy. The cornerstone of the new locks was laid on the Fourth of July, 1840.

Political infighting between a faction of Democrats, known as the Locofocos, and the emergent Whig Party in the legislature during Governor Seymour's administration led to the passage of a Stop Work Law in 1842 "to the dismay of the contractors," who suffered considerable financial losses. For the next four years, prominent men throughout Niagara County petitioned the canal commissioners to continue with the construction. Several contractors, including William Buell and Charles Hinman, continued to work, as a sign of good faith that they would eventually be paid. Another factor in the work stoppage was the national economic downturn or depression following the Panic of 1837.

In 1846, the Whigs in the legislature authorized the resumption of the work. But there were recriminations, charges, and counter-charges of fraud, waste, and incompetence leveled against Thomas Evershed, an engineer. An investigation was launched. Alexis Muller's account of the findings reported no specific charges, but the inquiry found evidence of "squandering of public funds in the construction of the locks at Lockport." Despite these setbacks and difficulties, including "reduced toll rates and increased railroad competition," however, the canal continued to prosper as receipts grew.

Later phases of the ongoing expansion and improvement of the canal continued to have an effect on the development of Lockport, including the final phase in the twentieth century, when Governor Theodore Roosevelt planned to save the canal system by transforming the Erie and its branches into the Barge Canal. It was at this stage that the five-tiered locks were replaced by a modern set of two hydraulic locks, Locks #34 & 35. The *Lockport Daily Journal* edition of November 22, 1909 reported on the transformation that took place in Lockport as a result of this project, in a tone reminiscent of the glory days of the 1820s:

> Stupendous is the word that adequately describes the Barge Canal work being done west of Lockport. It can confidently be asserted that it is one of the greatest engineering feats of modern times. From the Prospect Street Bridge westward every foot of the way is a veritable battleground with man against nature, a desperate fight between dynamite and machinery on one hand and century old rock on the other.

Signs on the horizon indicated that the canal was beginning to outlive its usefulness in the nineteenth century, particularly apparent with the coming of the railroad as the next revolution in America's transportation system. As something of a transportation hub, the railway came early to the village, developing parallel to the initial canal enlargement project. Muller's *Looking Back* booklet referred to the beginning of a "marriage between canal and rail that was to remain happy for only a few years." In its first years, the railway often picked up passengers directly from packet boats on the canal. And it was a sign of Lockport's continued economic advancement, as noted in the 1878 *History of Niagara County*:

> The opening of the railroad from Lockport to Niagara Falls, rude and imperfect as it was, did much toward giving an impetus to the business at Lockport . . . these facilities brought Lockport to the notice of capitalists from abroad.

Construction of the Lockport–Niagara Falls Strap Railway—one of the earliest railways in the nation—began in 1835. Built of strap iron laid on wooden rails, it was originally drawn by horses, but soon advanced to steam driven engines, in keeping with the transition from mules to steam boats on the canal. A famous episode from Lockport's popular history concerning this railroad, and Lockport's importance as a magnet for famous national figures on tour, occurred in September of 1839, when President Martin Van Buren made a stop in Lockport as part of a campaign trip through New York—the first time a president had visited the town. He was entertained by Washington Hunt at the Lockport House and the American Hotel with much fanfare, and spoke of seeing with the "liveliest satisfaction the improvements of Lockport" that were called to his attention, adding, for the sake of the voters, that these improvements were "mainly attributed" to internal improvements, "a work receiving from me an early, earnest and efficient support." In the course of traveling on the strap railway, one of the cars tipped over. President Van Buren proceeded to assist the other passengers in righting the car and returning it to the rails—and continued on his way to Niagara Falls.

The next advent of the railroad in Lockport occurred in 1852, when the Rochester, Lockport and Niagara Falls Railroad was up and running. Taking travelers and products beyond Niagara and into Genesee County broadened Lockport's horizons in many ways. A branch to Buffalo in Erie County was later added, and it was hailed as "a harbinger of deliverance from isolation and confinement" by some residents of the community.

The juxtaposition of the canal enlargement and the coming of the railroad evokes images of one of Lockport's most popular historical subjects—the abundance of bridges. From the articles of Clarence Lewis through the many commemorative publications and a recent program on the local PBS station, "Our Town—Lockport," the city's bridges have been a favorite topic for amateur historians and photographers alike. The refrain of the most well-known song associated with the canal, "Low Bridge, Everybody Down (Fifteen Years on the Erie Canal)" also points to the importance of bridges in the folklore of most canal towns. Obviously, building bridges—hundreds of them—was a necessity in the construction process all along the Erie, and some of Lockport's are legendary, prominently featured in postcards and photographs of the town and city from the early nineteenth century through the present.

Both Orsamus Turner and Joshua Wilber, two of Lockport's early chroniclers, wrote of a crude wooden structure that was Lockport's first bridge, built of logs. Wilbur indicated that the ride over it was very rough, as it was composed of "split logs, side by side, bark side up." In the early days, these bridges were often dangerous and the scene of accidents, which pointed to the need for increased safety measures in the enlargement projects. Recorded incidents include one notorious case in 1838, when a Mrs. Papworth was walking across Lockport's "high" or Gooding Street bridge over the canal in the heart of the town, with her two children. When the bridge collapsed, she had the presence of mind to toss the baby girl she was carrying onto the secure portion as she and her little boy fell. This mother's sacrifice saved both of the children, though she was killed.

Lockport's most famous bridge, now marked by a historic marker noting that it was "the world's widest bridge," is the "Big Bridge," first constructed of wood in 1858 across the full expanse of Main Street. It was transformed and replaced with an iron construction in 1868, and finally enlarged to include the Cottage Street Bridge as part of the Barge Canal expansion in 1914, when it could boast that it was one of the widest bridges in existence: 399 feet wide.

Lockport also has several rather unusual or atypical bridges still in existence, nostalgic reminders of bygone days. There are two "lift" bridges on Exchange and Adams Streets in Lowertown. Those traveling on a cruise down the canal are informed that one caretaker operates or lifts both bridges as required by passing boats The mechanical process is quite slow, allowing the caretaker to hop in his car and drive the short distance between the bridges to operate both in succession. The "upside down" or "railroad crossing" bridge is an intriguing visual oddity, and is a real landmark in Lockport. A railroad bridge constructed with the support trestle on the underside, it creates the illusion that it is upside down. Some of the best photographs of the canal locks have been taken from this bridge, making it serve as a link between the two modes of transportation so important to Lockport's history.

The Diversification of Industry Leads to Greater Prosperity and Progress

Even before the completion of the Erie Canal, the village of Lockport had established itself as a small business center, catering to the needs of the construction workers, engineers, and others who were attracted to the town because of its location. Land speculators were drawn to Lockport, and many ended up staying. The earliest enterprises, especially the numerous taverns and hotels, established fine reputations throughout the Niagara region. Contrary to the fears that Lockport would not survive after the canal was completed, it was transformed into something of a boom town, with early expectations that it would surpass Buffalo.

Early historical accounts are filled with lists of the number of businesses in operation at any given time, as proof that Lockport was a thriving community. An early popular history of Niagara County took an account of the multiplicity of mercantile and manufacturing establishments in the town in 1835, a decade after the opening of the canal. It includes assorted mills—Spalding's being the largest and most profitable in town—and a variety clothing and shoe stores, factories, iron foundries, machineries, tanneries, distilleries, blacksmith shops, jewelry stores, a printing office, and several newspapers. The overwhelming impression given by such lists was the phenomenal rate of Lockport's growth, and the diversification of its economic base. It was also becoming known as the flour center of western New York.

In several versions of the Clarence Lewis histories, 1844 was a banner year for taking stock, perhaps because such information was more readily available, or it was a favorable time to assess the progress of the town, after the coming of the first railway and the beginning of the enlargement work on the canal—the transportation network in place has always been a key indicator of Lockport's economic health. In "Synopsis of the History of Lockport, New York," Lewis offers the following rundown of businesses:

> 3 banks, 1 cotton factory, 1 woolen factory, 1 glass factory, 8 saw mills with
> 43 saws, 2 machine shops, 2 foundries, 2 tanning concerns, 1 piano factory,
> 2 gun factories, 1 last factory, 1 skin dressing plant, 1 patent fence factory, 1

bedstead factory, a brass factory, 1 sash factory, 4 cabinet shops, 22 dry goods stores, 15 groceries, 3 clothing stores, 4 hat, cap and fur shops, 2 window sash and paint stores, 3 book and stationary stores, 3 drug stores and several cooperages. 159,771 barrels of flour were manufactured in this year. 134,771 were shipped. Quarries sold over $60,000 in stone to Rochester and Buffalo.

Though very exhaustive, this account not only testifies to Lockport's robust economy, but sheds some light on the beginning of a cultural life in the town that had been a wilderness not so long ago. Progress was steady, in keeping with population growth. Lockport's population in the year 1840 was counted at 9,125.

The most memorable milestones and business establishments in Lockport's history include the founding of the first bank in Niagara County in 1829, the Bank of Lockport, with a charter secured by the Albany Land Company in hopes that the Lower Town would surpass the Upper Village. Industrially, it was already taking the lead. The Canal Bank in Upper Lockport was not opened until 1838. Rivalry between the two sections of town notwithstanding, banking was seen as "the helpmate of prosperity," and banks continued to be founded as the city grew, including the Exchange Bank in 1844, which was transformed into the Lockport office of the Manufacturers and Traders Trust Company of today, giving it claim to the title of the oldest bank in Niagara County.

Lockport gained an enviable reputation across the nation, as well as abroad, for its stone quarries, a logical outgrowth of the region's rich geologic resources and the valuable experience gained by local masons during the building of the locks. Niagara County's earliest histories noted the significance of these stone and marble interests: "Only next in importance to the great water power of Lockport are its inexhaustible stone quarries, which have attracted attention abroad and become a source of considerable wealth to the business interests of the city." The "splendid reputation of the quality" of Lockport limestone and Medina sandstone extended the reputation of the city and county, and was testified to by New York state geologists. Among the first quality stone quarries were those of Seth Whitmore, who arrived from Massachusetts in 1829 and bought acres of land on "Rattlesnake Hill," giving birth to a new variety christened "rattlesnake stone." C. B. Whitmore and B. & J. Carpenter also established quarries with the finest of reputations—Benjamin Carpenter parlayed his business reputation into politics, becoming the first mayor of the city of Lockport in 1865. Orders from as far away as New York City, Cleveland, and Chicago were placed with Lockport's quarries, and its stone was the preference of several Great Lakes cities when it came to constructing their municipal buildings and paving their main streets. Many of the finest homes in the city of Lockport, which still stand today thanks to recent historic preservation efforts, testify to this quality. In addition, the city hall and several churches of neighboring Buffalo were built of Lockport stone.

If Lockport won a fine reputation for its stone quarries, it also enjoyed the same when it came to its many taverns, which often played an important role in hosting visiting dignitaries. The first taverns, built in the 1820s, were the Lockport House, the Exchange Coffee House, the Black Eagle Tavern, and the Mansion House. Lyman

Spalding added another in 1833, first called the Central House but later known as the American. The most impressive and largest one in Lockport's early days was the Washington House, where General Lafayette was feted in 1825.

For a small town and city, Lockport has had a long and impressive record in publishing and newspapers, though frequent transformations and mergers make it difficult to keep the paper trail straight at times. A few examples should suffice to illustrate this point. As previously noted, Lockport's first newspaper was hijacked from neighboring Lewiston in 1821. When moved to Lockport, the *Niagara Democrat* became the *Lockport Observatory*, with Orsamus Turner serving as editor. The *Lewiston Sentinel* also moved to Lockport a short time later, and became the *Niagara Sentinel*. This paper and the *Observatory* were consolidated and published as the *Democrat & Sentinel*. In 1828 its name was changed by the new owner to the *Lockport Journal,* and again in 1829, when it became known as the *Lockport Balance*. The *Balance* merged with the *Gazette* briefly, but went back to the simple title of the *Lockport Balance.*

Turner started a new paper in 1835, which was transformed into a combination "*Niagara Democrat and Lockport Balance.*" There were other papers, short-lived, which served different purposes, such as Spalding's *Priestcraft Exposed,* and several advertising papers.

In 1859, a new weekly known as the *Lockport Chronicle* appeared, followed by the *Lockport Daily Union* in 1860. A series of further changes produced a new daily and new weekly paper in the city. The last phase of newspaper mergers and publications continued apace, with the eventual combination of three papers known as the *Lockport Union Sun & Journal* emerging in 1911. This paper has endured, in a sense, to the present day. However—following an all-too-common contemporary trend—it is part of a larger consortium in Niagara County, and its publication office is no longer located within the city limits.

In tandem with Lockport's growing diversified economic base, a major change regarding local government occurred in 1865, when Lockport advanced to a new stage and incorporated as the City of Lockport—the first city in Niagara County, with a population of 13,937. That watershed event, occurring near the middle of the century, serves as a pause for further consideration of Lockport's persistent progress in the nineteenth century—in civic spirit, culture, and business—with the flowering of two of its most famous enterprises, started by entrepreneurs with a flair for invention and marketing. These businesses enabled Lockport to scale new heights, and become distinctive as a center of ingenuity, thanks to a duo of colorful personalities, George Merchant and Birdsill Holly.

Ingenious Spirits Launch Unique Industries in the Lock City

More than any other "outside" author who has explored the history of Lockport, George Condon demonstrated a real appreciation of its unique qualities and colorful personalities, admiring it as a place that spawned and welcomed creative eccentrics. Chapters of his story of the Erie Canal, *Stars in the Water*, highlight the contributions of Merchant and Holly to Lockport lore, along with the obligatory section on the

"Seven Sutherland Sisters." These women, notorious for their breathtakingly long and abundant tresses (one boasted a length of seven feet!), found their fortune in hair tonic and as an act with the Barnum and Bailey circus in the late nineteenth century. But they were actually from Cambria, a town outside of Lockport, and they burned out quickly as a phenomenon with the coming of the twentieth century. The family was haunted by several tragic deaths and a spent fortune, but would always be remembered, in Condon's estimation, for a lot of hair: "perhaps more hair than ever has been concentrated in one family in American history."

More significant contributions to Lockport's business reputation and history were made by the manufacturing enterprises founded as Merchant's Gargling Oil and the Holly Manufacturing Company. Both of these establishments, in typical Lockport fashion, attracted the investment and participation of one of Lockport's leading figures, Washington Hunt. Dr. George Merchant was not only the inventor of a distinctive product, but Lockport's first advertising genius. Merchant's company was a favorite subject of the town's pioneer druggist and self-appointed historian, Joshua Wilber. Seeking his fortune in Lockport, he tried his hand at tailoring and printing, and finally purchased a drugstore at Market and Chapel Street in Lowertown, the site where Dr. Merchant's liniment was first manufactured.

In 1833, town pharmacist Merchant conducted some preliminary laboratory experiments and produced a medicine for the treatment of diseases that afflicted horses. A graduate of a Philadelphia college of pharmacy, Merchant also had a flair for the dramatic when it came to selling his "gargling oil." According to Condon, he put on the market "a product that would be a significant, influential factor in Lockport life for nearly a century." Although it was actually a liniment, and gargling it would have proven disastrous, it was an effective product:

> His timing was outstanding because as many of the Canal boats arrived at Lockport on their westward voyage, their horses and mules were pulling up lame as a result of the long, arduous hours on the towpath. Some of the canal hostlers tried Dr. Merchant's magic liniment with satisfactory results and the demand for the product began to grow.

For some reason, men in need of relief for their aching muscles began using the oil themselves, and sales soared. This led Dr. Merchant, who had formed a partnership with local store proprietor Morris Tucker, to build a new structure for the manufacture of his product. Over time, the business went through several transformations after Merchant's declining health led him to sell his share of the business. With Tucker, B. L. Delano and Henry Walbridge, Washington Hunt's father in law, formed a stock company to market the liniment. Under this new setup, Merchant's Gargling Oil entered its most prosperous years.

Condon gives credit for this phenomenal success to two factors: the infusion of new financial backing, and the sensational promotion techniques of Tucker, a "man ahead of his time." In 1850, for example, he sent a dozen bottles of the oil in an elaborately decorated box to the Sultan of Turkey, and "American newspapers publicized the hands-across-the-sea gesture" causing sales to skyrocket. Tucker also adopted the gargling oil's signature advertising slogan "Good for Man or Beast." Specific variations for men and beasts were produced, with grand labels. The oil for animals label featured an "Arabian stallion having his forelegs massaged by a turbaned groom," and "the oil for human use carried a label showing a man and his wife in an apparent state of felicity."

Another promotional genius and favorite son of Lockport, John Hodge, joined the company and became its president in 1881. He knew the value of "anywhere and everywhere" advertising, and had signs painted on "anything that would stand still along the entire length of the canal." It was "blatantly displayed on the side of the "Maid of the Mist" boat at Niagara Falls, which made that city's civic leaders "plainly wistful" when it "bobbed into view sporting banners that promoted an industry in rival Lockport." An even more spectacular feat was having an advertisement for Merchant's Gargling Oil painted on the Rock of Gibraltar!

Although sales waned in the twentieth century and the company died when its Market Street building burned in 1928, the company had enjoyed a great run, and contributed to Lockport's growing reputation well beyond the city and the state of New York. With the fortune he made in the business, John Hodge built Lockport's most famous cultural and entertainment center, the Hodge Opera House.

Birdsill Holly's achievements were even more far-reaching, and he easily qualifies as Lockport's most versatile, accomplished, and successful inventor, a man often considered to be in the same company as Thomas Edison. The town's popular historians have consistently taken great pride in Holly, and sung his praises in all of their works, often pointing to the frequent appearances of his inventions in displays and records at the Smithsonian Institution.

The Holly Manufacturing Company, more than any other single entity in Lockport history—with the exception of the canal—ties together so many of the pieces that constitute the chapters of the city's story: water power, distinction and renown beyond the city itself, and a fascinating person whose contribution made Lockport great.

Holly's two greatest contributions as an inventor were the Holly System of Water Works and Fire Protection and a system of central district steam heat. Born in Auburn in 1820, Birdsill Holly grew up in Seneca Falls, where he started his career as a machinist and worked in a variety of manufacturing concerns, earning over 150 patents for his inventions over his lifetime. These included important products like the elliptical rotary pump and the fire hydrant, which spurred him on to his great achievement in the field of fire prevention and safety. Holly was a visionary who thought big, and he was, in the final analysis, a man of systems rather than small parts. He came to Lockport in 1859, as an engineer for the Hydraulic Race Company, and supervised the work on the underground raceway tunnel, the major source of the surplus water power that transformed Lockport into an industrial center.

The most thorough treatment of this legend of Lockport was written by Madelynn P. Frederickson in 1996, *The Life and Times of Birdsill Holly*. Frederickson depicts Holly as one whose memory has never been properly honored. Despite his achievements and contributions, he never made his way into respectable Lockport society, owing largely to the fact that he divorced his first wife and married his young ward, creating quite a scandal in the town. And he never made a fortune from his work, generally moving on to some new venture just as the current one was becoming a financial success. Nevertheless, his was a momentous contribution to his adopted town, and his personal traits of "perseverance, genius, diligence and determination" help explain his great success as a gifted inventor with a practical spirit that served Lockport so well.

Holly's most visible imprint on the town appeared in the form of the Holly Manufacturing Company, which was located in a large, five story stone building constructed over the raceway in 1859 by the Manufacturers Building Company, an offshoot of the Lockport Hydraulic Race Company As he gained attention as a prolific inventor, Washington Hunt took notice of Holly and convinced him to move to Lockport.

Holly worked on several projects after arriving, including the manufacture of flat irons, the Holly Sewing Machine, and Holly's Patent Engine. Race Matthews, a recently formed Lockport company that produced steam fire engines, merged with Holly Manufacturing. This company, according to Frederickson, "brought wealth and prosperity to the community, employing more than 500 men in the industrial complex."

Birdsill Holly's remarkably inventive mind was a good match for Lockport at this critical time, five years after it had experienced its most devastating fire. The Holly System of Water Works would go a long way toward helping Lockport, and many other nineteenth century cities, fight the scourge of fires that afflicted so many communities. He had started in this field with a steam fire engine, which was entered in several competitions, impressing the judges in Brooklyn. In Lockport, he moved on to a pumping system network that would regulate a steady and constant flow of water for two purposes, providing water to both homes and fire hydrants. The final rendition of this system was known as the Holly System of Direct Pressure Water Supply and Fire Protection for Cities, Towns and Villages—all without the use of moveable engines. It constituted a significant technological improvement over Lockport's previous method of firing fires, the bucket brigade. Lockport was the pioneering city, and the Holly System was eventually adopted by 1,000 communities throughout the United States and Europe.

Initially his plans were met with skepticism, but Holly's dogged determination paid off for him, his adopted home, and for better fire protection for all the cities that followed Lockport's lead. Frederickson reports an interesting anecdote about Chicago in her manuscript, suggesting that the city's department of public safety recommended in 1868 that Holly's system be adopted by Chicago. Repeated delays, however, left the city unprotected in 1871 when the "worst fire in American history destroyed the city of Chicago."

This success led to plans to build a bigger complex in 1864 as the value of the company's stock doubled to $1,000, which encompassed a large site extending from

Gooding and Lock Streets, and Caledonia Street and the canal as the northern and southern boundaries. The tunnel for supplying the buildings with water power was excavated through the rock at the same time.

Holly's next major project again met with doubts about its feasibility, and he had to use his own home in Lockport, at 31 Chestnut Street, as the laboratory or testing ground for central steam heat. Persevering and using his own resources, he outfitted his home with a boiler and a system of pipes, extending them to his neighbor's house to demonstrate that his system could be used beyond a single home. Confident that the system would work, he gave up his role in the Holly Manufacturing Company to concentrate on the Holly Steam Combination Company in 1877. The City of Lockport gave the company a franchise, and it was extended to serve major portions of the city. The following year, plants were installed at Auburn; Garden City, Long Island; and at a Soldier's Home in Dayton, Ohio. Once again Lockport was a trendsetter, as other cities sent committees to investigate the system, now up and running successfully. After some minor problems were worked out, the name was changed to the American District Steam Company in 1881, and it caught on like wildfire in over 35 states and Canada.

One grand dream of Holly's was unsuccessful—the idea of building a skyscraper on Goat Island at Niagara Falls. Toward the end of his life he was moving toward active involvement in the aluminum industry, also born in Lockport. But he became seriously ill in 1893 and died in 1894. The eulogist at his funeral spoke of "the great good to the world resulting from his active life," and one of the local newspapers printed a tribute from the Holly Manufacturing Company, which stated in part:

> That by his greatness and skill he has developed many inventions in the line of mechanic arts which have been of great benefit to humanity . . . the success which has attended the operations of this Company . . . is largely due to his skill as an inventor and engineer . . . the Holly System of Water Supply and Fire Protections . . . has been extensively imitated throughout the civilized world by other builders and engineers.

It was quite a testimonial to the deceased, a man who had brought honor and great wealth to Lockport.

Birdsill Holly's legacy lived on in Lockport in the form of his Holly Manufacturing complex, but not permanently. In another twist of the fate that seemed to bedevil his life periodically, a bitter labor strike in 1901 inflicted damage from which it was never able to recover, and the Holly Foundry was moved to Buffalo. A final irony was the destruction by fire of the old Holly Building, which spread to the Holly Manufacturing complex and destroyed one of Lockport's greatest landmarks.

Persistent Fires and an Indomitable Civic Spirit

In the course of writing about the city's lore and ingenious entrepreneurs, George F. Condon observed that "there was hardly ever a dull year in the long history of Lockport." This was most close to the truth during the nineteenth century, and especially germane to one of the most persistent and pervasive phenomena recorded in all the city's annals—the ever present threat of damaging fires, which occurred on a regular basis. A person exploring the story of Lockport's past would note this immediately, as the theme of repeated fires and the damages suffered emerges as a continuous thread in Lockport's history. It was a recurrent fear, particularly in the days when most of the town's structures were built of wood. Despite the fact that no lives were lost in these fires, they take on the air of a plague of almost Biblical proportions in the pages of Lockport's recorded past.

The most memorable fire—the "great" fire in Lockport's history—occurred on the night of November 2, 1854. It was described by Clarence Lewis as the town's "first really disastrous and spectacular fire." Starting in the Lockport House, it spread to the north and the east, raging beyond the capability of the town's bucket brigades. It was finally extinguished thanks to the "aid of two fire engines brought from Buffalo on flat cars on the railroad" and a speedy response from Erie, Pennsylvania to an SOS telegram—but not before inflicting extensive damage. Three hotels, eighteen stores, eight houses, a barn, and two churches—the Congregational and the Methodist—were consumed. In addition, it was the first of two fires that would have long-term ill effects as far as future historians were concerned, as it destroyed many of the town's records. The account in the 1878 popular history of Niagara County reported that the village was "visited with a destructive fire" on that awful night—the "most extensive and disastrous conflagration that ever occurred in Lockport." But it did not destroy the community's spirit, and proved to be the first of many such tragic fires that only led the townspeople to pick up the pieces and move on with a firm resolution to keep their eyes fixed on the promise of the future: "The loss was severe, but not withstanding the discouraging outlook, the debris was soon removed and the cheerless scene enlivened by men employed in erecting other structures upon the same foundations."s

Hope would spring eternal after most of the fires, evidence of the spirit of optimism that prevailed in the community. The essence of Lockport's long-term story is one of periodic setbacks interspersed with moments of triumph in the steady march of progress. In the face of many challenges posed by new industrial and technological innovations, Lockport managed to maintain a healthy sense of balance—a reflection of the American national spirit.

Lockport remained an attractive site for visitors, including the prominent from all walks of life. Henry Clay, the Great Compromiser, had visited in 1839. Like President Van Buren, he was impressed with the famous locks and the rising tide of prosperity so obvious in the town. In 1843, former President John Quincy Adams stopped in Niagara County and spoke of Lockport as "classic ground" where the ten combined locks are located: "there the famous Morgan trials were held and McLeod was imprisoned." Winfield Scott, general turned presidential candidate, arrived in 1852, and a reporter noted that "great changes had indeed been wrought since he had periled his life in repelling the enemy upon the Niagara frontier. The canal was only an enterprise contemplated in the future, and Lockport was an unbroken wilderness." General Scott alluded to the canal as a "monument of lasting fame:" "The rapid changes which seem to mark your onward progress are truly astonishing. Indeed, to know and appreciate your position, it would seem necessary to pay you a visit every few years." It was clear that most visitors were struck by the speed and significance of change in Lockport.

Technology was another frequent visitor to Lockport. The town was often at the beginning of the itinerary as these cutting-edge scientific improvements traversed the nation. For example, the first communal telegraph line was laid between Buffalo and Lockport in 1844. The Gas and Light Company of Lockport was established in 1851, followed by the coming of telephone service in 1879. Electric lights replaced gas lamps on Main Street starting in 1885.

Innovations in travel, befitting a city grounded in transportation, also appeared in quick succession: the Horse Car Railway in 1886 and the Lock City Electric Railway in 1892, which proved to be the source of much consternation when the entire railway was stolen and carried away on flat cars. Charles K. Lawrence, the construction manager with a penchant for larceny, bribed some trainmen to attach a switch engine to the cars. He was apprehended and sentenced to a term in the Auburn State Prison.

The Union Station railroad depot, one of Lockport's most treasured architectural landmarks, was built in 1888—only to be destroyed by fire in 1978. By 1896, regular trolley service was established, and in 1900, electric cars ran to Olcott Beach, a popular resort town on Lake Ontario. The Rochester, Lockport and Buffalo line was in operation four years later, expanding the town's outlook even further.

As proof of its patriotism and obligation to the nation, Lockport sent its sons to war when America called. Clarence Lewis's column of May 28,1953, relates the claim that a "Lockport Man Was First to Volunteer for Civil War." After the Battle of Fort Sumter was covered in the Lockport newspapers, local citizen William W. Bush, proprietor of the Oyster Saloon, posted a notice in town on April 15, 1861, "announcing that he was recruiting a company for the impending war."

Because this was done before President Lincoln's call for volunteers had been received in Lockport, "by this premature patriotic act, W. W. Bush . . . became the first volunteer for the Civil War in the United States." The company, composed of 83 men who responded to his initial notice, became part of the 28th regiment of New York State. The town staged a massive celebration for them, staging a parade at the Court House and suspending all village business as it sent its sons marching off to war.

World War I produced a local hero in Frank J. Gaffney, who was recognized for his bravery in battle in 1918. Assuming command of his platoon after his lieutenant and sergeant were killed, Private Gaffney reached the objective, a German machine gun nest, killing several of the enemy soldiers and capturing more as prisoners of war. General Pershing himself considered him the second greatest hero of the war. In the 1950s, a street constructed between Transit and Pine Streets was named Gaffney Road to honor him. After World War I ended, local artist Raphael Beck designed a monument to honor the memory of Lockport's veterans. Completed in 1930, the Soldiers and Sailors Monument was later renamed the Lockport War Memorial and serves as the centerpiece of the site on East Avenue now known as Veterans Memorial Park. It includes the names of Lockportians who lost their lives in defense of their country in both world wars, as well as the conflicts in Korea and Vietnam.

During the period following the Civil War through the early twentieth century, fires reappeared with greater frequency in the city. On July 17, 1865, the *Lockport Daily Journal* carried a "Conflagration in Lockport" headline. Once again, citizens had been "alarmed by the cries of fire" in the night. Starting in a barn connected to the old Washington House, the "flames spread with astonishing rapidity." The Washington House—"among the oldest buildings in the city . . . for some time it was *the* hotel of the place"—was completely destroyed, along with a blacksmith shop and two homes. Although the fire companies promptly responded to the call and managed to save some buildings, the loss of the landmark Washington House was a difficult one for the city to bear. The paper editorialized that it should serve as a "wake up call" for the city to come up with a better way of fighting fires with "insufficient hose" that led to the "uncalled for sacrifice of property." The call would be most ably answered by Birdsill Holly, whose system prevented some future losses, though it could hardly be expected to eliminate the threat posed by fires. More destructive fires appeared in the following decades. The new Hodge Opera House, one of Lockport's finest structures, was a casualty of Lockport's next big fire in 1881. Hodge promptly rebuilt his structure, a center of Lockport entertainment and commerce. At the time of the fire, the Hodge House was also the location of many professional offices, the post office, a newspaper office, and the city clerk's office. The loss of the vital statistical records of the city was irreparable.

In 1899, St Mary's German Catholic Church was the victim of a fire and had to be rebuilt. In 1909, as Clarence Lewis told it, "Lockport suffered two disastrous fires" that were compounded by a recession, causing Lockport's population to stagnate after steadily rising since the 1830s. A frequent visitor to Market Street structures, the fires destroyed the Boston and Lockport Block Factory and the Holly Manufacturing Company building, another great landmark.

In February of 1928, "lightning struck twice" when the Hodge Opera House fell victim to a second round of fire, this one sounding the death knell of the historic building. The headline in the *Union-Sun & Journal* read "Entire Business District Threatened." The blaze also gutted the Merchant's Gargling Oil building, where it started. It took firefighters from Lockport, Buffalo, Medina, Newfane, and Niagara Falls "some 17 hours to douse the blaze." The damage was estimated at $350,000. This spectacular fire brought an end to a form of high culture in the city, as the Bewley Office Building, which still stands, was built in 1929 on the opera house's surviving foundation.

Along with progress in business and industry, Lockport enjoyed a vibrant cultural and community life during these years. The highlight of this cultural development, which brought national attention and many famous entertainers and civic leaders to the city, was the Hodge Opera House. In all historical retrospectives of Lockport's heritage and culture, it is the most commanding presence. A special edition of the *Union-Sun & Journal* was published in 1965 to commemorate Lockport's 100th anniversary as a city, and included an article entitled "Community Took Pride in the Old Opera House." It bordered on the hagiographic, with comparisons to "the grandeur that was Greece and the glory that was Rome . . . which for forty years was the entertainment, cultural and civic center of Lockport."

It was erected in 1871 by John Hodge with the fortune he amassed as president of Merchant's Gargling Oil, once "the biggest and most prosperous business of the city"—partially as an attempt to give something back to the city. The first and second floors housed various offices, public and private, as well as lodge rooms of local fraternal organizations such as the Eagles, Moose, and the Ancient Order of Hibernians. It was the third floor that garnered the most favorable attention as one of the finest structures of its kind in the state. It featured a large auditorium that seated 2,000 people and included an orchestra pit and a large stage. It was so large, according to a recent article by Clarence "Dutch" Adams of the Niagara County Historical Society, "that New York City big theatrical productions would stop in Lockport before going on to Buffalo." It could accommodate horses and even elephants for its grandest performances. During its 40-year existence, many famous national figures graced its stage as lecturers and performers. The most renowned included feminists Susan B. Anthony and Elizabeth Cady Stanton, soldier-statesman General Benjamin Butler, Horace Greeley, Oliver Wendell Holmes, P. T. Barnum, and Thomas Nast. The Reverend Henry Ward Beecher, according to Lewis, "held his audience spellbound" there. And the great champion boxer John L. Sullivan fought on the Hodge House stage in the 1890s, as part of a production of "The Man From Boston."

The structure itself was extravagant and grand in its design, accordning to local student of Lockport history John P. Hicks Jr. A 38-foot high dome featured portraits of Presidents Washington, Jefferson, Lincoln, and Garfield, other famous Americans, and Shakespeare, Goethe, and Schiller. Frescoes of classical muses also adorned the building and a "vivid scene of the Grand Canal in Venice" appeared on its curtain. With the final destruction of the Hodge Opera House, a cultural era in Lockport came to an end. Other fine theatres would be built in Lockport, such as the Rialto, the Majestic, and the Palace, but nothing to compare to the one-of-a-kind opera house that John Hodge built—twice.

Transitions

Coming full circle, and returning to the focus on business and industry as indicative of Lockport's steady climb up the ladder of economic success and civic progress, the year 1910 marked a change in Lockport's status and outlook that would have important repercussions throughout the century. It was in this year that three new companies established themselves as the major industries of twentieth century Lockport: Simonds Saw and Steel Company, which built a local plant in the city; the Upson Company; and the Harrison Radiator Company.

A history of Lockport's settlement and growth prepared by the eastern Niagara Chamber of Commerce in 1979, "Lockport—To the Canal and Beyond," noted the importance of this influx of new industries: "the business acquisitions of 1910 spearheaded Lockport's move into the twentieth century." The two local founders, Charles A. Upson and Herbert Champion Harrison, would become community leaders whose names and memories have been permanently preserved in the annals of Lockport history. And it was in 1910 that the community custom of Old Home Week started, a sign that future generations would find a key to a prosperous future in preserving Lockport's glorious past.

Chapter Eight

HOPE IN THE HISTORY

Lockport is situated on the Mountain Ridge, and there are here five double locks of twelve feet lift each, situated a few yards below the village . . . constructed in the most permanent manner, and the science and solidity displayed by them has often been spoken of with admiration. There are stone steps between the rows of locks, guarded on each side with iron railings. This is the most stupendous work on the whole route.
                                                          —*The Tourist Pocket Manual,*1838

Today's Lockport is struggling to regain that confidence. The 1970s left an unhappy architectural legacy, and the downtown is pockmarked with abandoned buildings and dusty businesses. But the town has not given up and is vigorously using the draw of the Famous Five to lure tourists. A new Visitors Center provides good maps and a bit of local history; the canal banks are neatly planted and maintained, and a boat service offers guided tours of the locks, while trolley tours rumble through the leafy older bits of town.
                        —Cait Murphy and Rosanne Haggerty, "The Erie Rising," 2001

A retrospective glance at the panorama of Lockport's history reveals a somewhat harsh truth—that the twentieth century has not been as kind to the city as the nineteenth century had been. Over time, the spotlight shining on Lockport began to fade, and its fortunes waned as a result of a changing national economy and an unsuccessful experiment with urban renewal during the 1960s. Of the three industrial companies that came to Lockport in 1910, only one survives, having undergone several transformations. Both the Simonds Saw and Steel plant and the Upson Company are gone. Harrison Radiator, once a division of the General Motors Corporation, is now Delphi Harrison Thermal Systems, and remains the region's largest employer.

But a study of Lockport's past also reveals another valuable lesson—that it has managed to come back time and again, like a phoenix rising from the ashes, particularly after a succession of destructive fires. A persistent theme that has endured in the face of multiple changes and challenges is Lockport's ever-expectant spirit, resolute in the face of adversity and now hopeful about the positive signs on the horizon at the dawn of the twenty-first century.

Economic Changes and the Sad Saga of Urban Renewal

With the arrival of the three large manufacturing firms at the beginning of the twentieth century, Lockport's economy went through yet another transition, and weathered the changes well. Simonds, one of the largest industries to move to Lockport after the loss of the Holly Manufacturing Company, located a plant on Ohio Street, which produced steel and related specialty products and became a major source of employment in western New York. Historian Clarence Lewis noted that the City of Smokeless Power was expanding its industrial might in its "most spectacular year since the turn of the century."

The Upson Company was founded by two brothers, Charles A. and W. H. Upson Jr. According to the company brochure celebrating its 45th anniversary, the brothers had been associated with the old Niagara Paper Mill of Lockport, but struck off on their own after "conceiving the idea of establishing a plant for the manufacture of a better and more dependable wallboard than was being produced in those days." The first plant was located in Lowertown, in a building of importance in Lockport's early history. It had originally housed a cotton factory and was purchased by Governor Washington Hunt in 1841. In 1857, he and his partners converted it into a flour mill, powered by the surplus waters from the raceway. Like many of Lockport's historic buildings, it was swept by fire and the surviving structure housed the Old Franklin Mills.

In a pattern characteristic of Lockport industry during the last century, the Upson Company prospered and expanded, moving to a new location on Stevens Street in 1914. The company produced a quality wallboard—"strong, fire-resisting, waterproofed"—which was in high demand by the war department, and shipped overseas for the construction of servicemen's housing. The company also branched off in new directions, producing jigsaw puzzles during the depression, creating the TUCO division. Like many companies, it struggled to keep up with the demands of modernization during the 1970s. A planned expansion suffered from delays of delivery of new equipment, a decline in demand for its product, and a labor strike. By the 1980s, the homegrown company filed for bankruptcy, and was sold off in pieces to other companies—a surviving remnant, in the form of Niagara Fiberboard Inc., remained in a building on the bank of the canal in Lowertown, but the dominance of the Upson Company was over. The memory of founding brother Charles A. Upson lives on permanently in Lockport, in terms of his service as the first president of the Rotary Club and other civic contributions to the city. One of the city's elementary schools is named after him.

The company that had the greatest impact on Lockport was founded by Herbert Champion Harrison. Born in India, Harrison earned a degree in electrical engineering from Trinity College at Oxford University before coming to the United States in 1907. He was one of the organizers of the Susquehannah Smelting Company, which was bought out by the Union Carbide Corporation. The local biography file at the Lockport Public Library notes that it was during this phase of his career that his interest in automobile radiators was sparked, and he designed the Harrison Hexagon Radiator, with its honeycomb appearance. His Harrison Radiator Company grew by leaps and bounds, becoming the anchor of Lockport industry—both yesterday and today. During the height of its operation, it occupied two buildings—the downtown plant on Walnut Street, and the larger "west end" plant in the town—today, only the west end plant remains in operation as the world headquarters of the company that started almost a century ago.

Harrison became part of the General Motors Corporation in 1918, and diversified its product line to include heating and cooling systems in addition to the original radiators. A 1999 press release from the company (no longer affiliated with General Motors) in its current incarnation, Delphi-Harrison, noted that it remained "a powerful economic force on the local economy." In fact, consensus opinion in the city and town of Lockport agrees that it is the foundation of the region's economy—all the more important since the decline of the Lockport commercial and retail downtown area.

The decline of downtown is the major story in Lockport's recent history—it has loomed like a dark cloud over the city, physically in terms of the stagnant eyesore known as the South Block, and mentally in the minds of generations who still remember a vibrant and lively downtown shopping district, attracting people from all over Niagara County before the days of urban renewal. As with many communities, suburban malls and the "Wal-Mart style" of shopping have had an ill effect on traditional downtown areas that are often built on family-owned establishments. But Lockport's story is further complicated by a lengthy tale involving the clash of politicians and strong-willed developers, and decades of legal battles—all working to the detriment of the city and its inhabitants.

The sad story has been told many times, from a variety of perspectives, but one of the most succinct and objective versions can be found in a four part series written by David R. Kinyon for the Lockport *Union-sun & Journal* in September of 1990, while he served as president of the Chamber of Commerce. Kinyon's purpose was to review the failures of the past, while still looking positively to the future, hopeful that things could and would change.

Earlier renditions of the story noted that the urban renewal project in Lockport grew out of the national movement associated with the Johnson administration's "Great Society." The plan in Lockport called first for the restoration of a blighted Lowertown in the early 1960s—"hope for a bad neighborhood"—with the infusion of state and federal funding. But the focus shifted to an emphasis on modernizing downtown first, and disagreements on how best to proceed toppled several mayors, Democrat and Republican alike, in the see-saw style of small town politics.

Money and attention focused on Main Street, which has nevertheless languished for decades. Community spirit in Lowertown, on the other hand, has successfully improved that area of the city, with a major emphasis on historic preservation of old stone buildings and the building of a canal walkway and park near the Widewaters Marina and up the Market Street hill.

An earlier series in the local newspaper—indicative of the fact that the decline of downtown has been a perennial favorite headline, bordering on obsession, for the past three decades—wrote of disagreements over funding sources, bond issues, geographical scope of the project, and emphasis: hotel-motel complex and/or a revived retail center or mall. By 1966, Mayor Rollin T. Grant was speaking about "the rebirth of our city"—a particularly bitter sentiment for contemporary Lockportians, who know all too well that this dream has been deferred repeatedly since that time, and never fulfilled during the past 40 years. The juxtaposition of outlooks, from earlier hopeful days and the recent dismal reality, illustrate the truth of the thesis stated at the beginning of this chapter—that Lockport's image has waned since its nineteenth century heyday. A reference in an old city directory from 1924 is particularly striking when contrasted with more contemporary times. A notation of a fund of $60,000 provided by the Lockport Improvement Corporation "to cover the only unsightly spot on Main Street" evokes bittersweet memories of the old days. The writer of this entry in the directory went on to see this as "evidence of the right spirit and the way Lockport does things," and anyone with a long-term perspective can only hope that that "right spirit" is on the rise again in Lockport.

Kinyon's series focused on the "City's South Block: History of No Action." The situation in 1972 was one of the major structures being razed, and an almost war-torn downtown waiting to be rebuilt. The cornerstone of the section of Main Street between Locust and Pearl Alley/Heritage Court—Lockport's "fabled million dollar block"—the most lucrative piece of commercial real estate in downtown Lockport, with a market value of a staggering one million dollars"—was Williams Brothers Department Store, located at 78 Main Street. Founded in 1879, it enjoyed a well-earned reputation as "the style and shopping center of Niagara County," featuring quality clothing. But once Williams Brothers closed its doors as part of the renewal plan, "it was never to reopen again in downtown Lockport." Residents have looked forward to the "hoped for renaissance of their cherished community gathering spot" in vain. In Kinyon's words, "the renaissance of downtown Lockport has never evolved as had been hoped for"—a statement that remained true for over a decade after his articles were published.

There was some new construction downtown by various developers working with the Lockport Urban Renewal Agency, including Lockview Plaza and Heritage Square and the former Bassett Travel Agency and Greyhound Bus terminal at Elm and Walnut Streets. This last project brought local developer Elmer Granchelli to the center stage, with plans for what was hoped to be the crowning jewel in downtown Lockport's urban renewal dream. His proposal was for a 70,000 square foot office/retail complex, anchored by the Manufacturers Hanover Bank of New York City, to be called Manor Mall. But, despite several revisions in the plan and a name change to Regency Row, all of these plans have failed, and produced nothing but years of litigation, finger-pointing, and blame between Granchelli and city officials, and the always stark reminder of the failure—a blighted center block in the heart of downtown.

As time went on and no progress was made, other factors made it less likely that downtown could be resuscitated. By the 1980s, competing shopping malls had been constructed, in Erie County and in the town of Lockport. A major rezoning issue, for a professional office park in the town of Lockport, proved to be a watershed mark for Granchelli, and created more ill will between the developer and city officials. Multiple lawsuits arose, with accusations that the city was acting in bad faith countered by the city's threats to repossess the property due to the developer's failure to build. As time passed, the weeds continued to grow on the South Block, and the city's optimism about any change occurring here dimmed. Another local developer, David Ulrich, emerged as a player in the high stakes game for Lockport's future, and he was a major force behind the construction on Davison Road and the Triangle Plaza downtown. One of the conclusions arrived at by Kinyon was that the South Block Plan had been hurt by these numerous disputes, and the slide down the slippery slope of decline continued throughout the 1990s.

A 1996 article in Buffalo's *Business First*, "Granchelli Empire Dominates Downtown Lockport," underscored the role that strong personalities played in the lengthy impasse. Reporter Thomas Hartley wrote of the relationship between the developer and the city: "like new marriage partners, Elmer Granchelli and Lockport launched their new relationship full of hope, vision and enthusiasm." But eventually "hard feelings and recriminations replaced the rosiness of earlier years."

Sadly, the major casualty was the city—where for "more than 100 years" downtown was the heart of Lockport. Its proud history of progress was badly damaged as 12 mayoral administrations proved unequal to the challenge:

> Today, it is still what it was in 1974—a forlorn, barren, weedy plot of ground. The lack of development has cost the city $700,000 in lost tax dollars. . . . It created the impression that Lockport was powerless to control its future . . . and it dimmed the reputation of some of the participants

In a follow-up piece written in 2002, Hartley focused on David Ulrich's efforts in "trying to ensure a healthy Lockport." The tone was one of the passing of the torch to a younger generation, the clash of the titans winding down. Granchelli was no longer the sole dominant force in downtown Lockport, as Ulrich had expanded his family's insurance business and launched the Ulrich Development Company. His holdings included the Professional Park on Davison Road and many historic bank buildings downtown, with a self-proclaimed focus on "returning Main Street to its grandeur . . . my goal in revitalizing Main Street is the revitalization of the city." Some progress was being made, but the South Block remained the stumbling block.

Very recently, however, there has been a reversal of fortunes. After years of legal wrangling, the city was able to regain control of this property after winning a breach of contract suit. Mayor Michael Tucker announced plans for a grand project on July 15, 2004 after the city reached an agreement with developer Ulrich. The front page article in the *Union-Sun & Journal* by Joyce M. Miles reported on "a vision of South Block as 'City Centre,' an elegant mix of form, function and meaning." Ulrich's plans called for a four point development project: retail and office space, a professionally operated farmers market, and a heritage park. The park would celebrate Lockport's ordinary citizens "who make the city what it was, what it is, and what it can be," allowing families to plant time capsules to be opened in the future, by later generations of these same hardy folk who are the heart and backbone of the community. Ulrich also noted that his City Centre would proceed with the reconstruction of Main Street, with an eye toward "making a walk down Main Street a walk through history." A story in *The Buffalo News* was written with a guarded "air of optimism . . . optimism that after 28 years of failure and frustration David L. Ulrich will put an end to the gaping hole in the heart of Lockport's downtown business district."

Thomas Hartley's article on this long-overdue announcement of changing times was entitled "Renaissance for Downtown Lockport." A frank summary of the sad reality of Lockport's recent history—"decades of failed promises and false starts . . . and the residents who have "long hoped for a project to jump-start a dead downtown that was written off when urban renewal ripped out its heart 40 years ago"—gave way to a hopeful historical perspective on brighter days ahead.

This sense that a respect for history offered the way out of Lockport's twentieth century wilderness is especially fitting, and was underscored by references to a unique arched passageway as part of the Heritage Park. This feature would recreate the arches of Union Station, "Lockport's picturesque and beloved 19th century railroad station now lying in ruins from a fire." Echoes of Lockport's glorious past resonate in these plans. Despite the fact that previous Union Station restoration plans never came to fruition, a piece of this part of Lockport's history will be revived in the promising City Centre Project. It is almost as if Clio, the muse of history, has a hand in the work going on in contemporary Lockport, guiding those seeking to reclaim the city's heritage as the key to making the most of its future.

Famous Sons and Daughters: Lockport's Contribution to the Wider World

A common characteristic of many small towns is the pride they take in their own citizens who go on to achieve fame and acclaim. It reflects well on the town and its values, it is thought—the role of luck is seldom considered, for the community likes to think it had something to do with the accomplishments of its favorite sons and daughters. Lockport is no exception in this regard. A brief exploration of a representative sample of its most prominent people, from all walks of life throughout its history, should serve to illustrate this point.

The contributions of several of Lockport's inventors and businessmen have already been noted: Lyman Spalding, Birdsill Holly, and Herbert Champion Harrison. Washington Hunt was surely the town's most famous nineteenth century political figure. Governor Hunt was revered throughout his life, and mourned in grand style on the occasion of his death in 1867 when the obituary in the *Niagara Democrat* noted that the telegram announcing his death "fell like a pall upon the hearts of the citizens of Lockport." In addition to his political accomplishments, he was remembered for his civic contributions to the town after he returned home when his political career was over, and as a leading businessman and member of the Episcopal Church. His legacy lives on in the form of the Wyndham Lawn Home for Children on Old Niagara Road. Once his private estate, it was turned over to the community first as the Home of the Friendless. A Lockport elementary school is also named after him. The obituary summed up his place in Lockport's history by underscoring the prevailing sense of loss expressed for "the most eminent, honored and best beloved fellow citizen and neighbor"

Another nineteenth century political figure and educator was Belva Lockwood. Born on a farm in the Niagara County town of Royalton in 1830, she served as the preceptor of Lockport's Union School before going on to become the first female lawyer to argue before the Supreme Court. Her greatest notoriety stemmed from the fact that she was the first woman to run for president. In 1884 and again in 1888 she ran as the candidate of the National Equal Rights Party in an effort to advance women's rights

Raphael Beck (1858–1947) was one of Lockport's most famous artists, beloved and remembered locally for his 1925 mural commissioned by the Lockport Exchange Bank, "The Opening of the Erie Canal, October 26, 1953." It depicts Lockport's finest moment, when Governor De Witt Clinton came to the town and passed through the flight of five locks. The son of accomplished artist Augustus Beck, he was born in Pennsylvania and later settled in Lockport and built a studio in Buffalo. Each year on his birthday he performed the ritual of walking the 23 miles to his office in Buffalo from his home on Lockport's Willow Street. Beck's fame reached well beyond the environs of Lockport, most notably for his design of the logos of the Pan-American Expositions. He painted the last portrait of President William McKinley, shortly before he was assassinated in Buffalo while visiting the Exposition in Buffalo in 1901. Beck also designed Lockport's Soldiers Monument or War Memorial, and is buried at Lockport's Glenwood Cemetery.

O. C. (Othniel Charles) Marsh was one of the most highly respected paleontologists of the nineteenth century. Born in Lockport in 1851, he began his study of geology and fossils in the fields of western New York, and went on to prominence as the president of the National Academy of Sciences and endowed professor of paleontology at Yale University. His education and the Peabody Museum of Paleontology at Yale were funded by his uncle, George Peabody. He published *The Dinosaurs of North America* in 1895. In an article written for the "Sunday Magazine" of the *Buffalo News*, "O. C. Marsh: New York's Pioneer Fossil Hunter," Matthew Riley argued that his interest in science was a logical outgrowth of the hometown environment, and that "through a lifetime of study, struggle and discovery, O. C. Marsh's scientific adventures led him on a hard, unlikely path that started on the banks of the Erie Canal."

A man who had a great impact on Lockport in terms of his contributions to the arts is William Rand Kenan. A businessman turned philanthropist, Kenan was born in Wilmington, North Carolina in 1872 and moved to Lockport in 1900. He made his fortune from the discovery and production of calcium carbide, and formed the Union Carbon and Carbide Corporation at Niagara Falls, New York and the Western Block Company of Lockport. A millionaire in the best Horatio Alger tradition, Kenan assumed an active role in Lockport's community life. A pillar of Lockport's First Presbyterian Church, he willed his home, a stately mansion on Locust Street, to the church. It remains a permanent testimonial to his philanthropic work, and serves as Lockport's cultural center today. Reporter Nancy A. Fischer, writing about the Kenan Center in *The Buffalo News* in 2001, called it a center of attractions: the 25 acre campus serves as "a haven for art and theatre. A flower lover's paradise. A recreation center and preschool for children. A site rich with museum-quality history."

Though often forgotten and unrecognized outside of the community, William E. Miller was the Lockport politician who scaled the highest heights, becoming Barry Goldwater's running mate on the Republican presidential ticket in the election of 1964. A relatively obscure congressman before he was catapulted to a spot in the national limelight, Miller had served as convention chairman when Goldwater chose him. His Catholic faith and western New York roots were perceived as a good balance for Arizona's Goldwater.

Lockport was thrilled at the achievement of its favorite political son, and local newspapers carried headlines about Miller, many of them going overboard in the interest of hometown pride: "Lockport Residents are Proud of Miller," "Miller Outshines Other County Political Giants," and "September 5, 1964 Was the Greatest Day in the City's Political History" (an early editorial had proclaimed that date Bill Miller Day in Lockport). Even after the Republicans were defeated by a real "Landslide Lyndon" victory on the part of President Johnson and Hubert H. Humphrey, the city remained proud that one of its own had risen to such high status.

Upon Miller's death in 1983, he was eulogized in glowing terms, as the highlights of his illustrious career were recalled: a graduate of the University of Notre Dame, he had served as legal counsel during the Nuremberg war crime trials before becoming a congressman in 1950. After retiring from political life, he came home to Lockport with his family, resumed his private law practice, and became an active member of the community, serving on several boards and working as a director of the Niagara Frontier Transportation Authority. Barry Goldwater said that the greatest lesson he had learned form his running mate was that "your country comes first." William Miller was buried with full military honors in Arlington National Cemetery.

One of America's most prolific and celebrated authors, Joyce Carol Oates, also traces her roots back to Lockport, or the small settlement by the Tonawanda Creek in Erie County, Millersport. Winner of the National Book Award and a professor of humanities at Princeton University, Oates has traveled far from home, but acknowledges the role that her early childhood played in her novels, and the attraction of western New York as a setting for many of her stories. In an article in the *New York Times Magazine* in 1989, "My Father, My Fiction," Oates wrote that "my writing is, at least in part, an attempt to memorialize my parents' vanished world; my parents' lives." *You Must Remember This* (1987) is set in a "mythical western New York city that is an amalgam of Buffalo and Lockport, but primarily Lockport: the novel could not have been imaginatively launched without the Erie Canal . . . cutting through its core." The opening chapters of another novel, *Wonderland* (1971), are set in Lockport, where the protagonist Jesse finds himself "fascinated by the bridges and the canal in Lockport" after being adopted by a family there. One of her poems, from *Angel Fire* (1973), is entitled "City of Locks," and is most evocative of Lockport's history:

> "the world's largest single span bridge"
> is jumbled today with shoppers' cars
> along this mile of the Erie Barge Canal
> there are juttings of rock long blasted out
>
> at Lockport, New York, at the famous locks
> there are rusted railings painted over . . .
>
> eye to eye with the broken windows of warehouses
> across the canal
> we wait
> wait for something to become clear—
> but nothing happens
> in these meager cities of our childhoods
> nothing is declared

Written at a low point in Lockport's history, this poem exhibits a depressing outlook—it was during this period that nothing was happening in terms of rebuilding the heart of the city. But, change is finally in the air in 2005, and the future clearly looks brighter than Oates thought 30 years ago.

Hope Springs Eternal

In addition to the progress being made downtown with the construction of the City Centre, there have been other signs that things are looking up in Lockport with respect to taking full advantage of the Erie Canal's potential and the city's rich history. It has long been common wisdom, supported by the recommendations of "experts" in urban planning and tourism, that the city of Lockport was not making the best use of the resources available and in close proximity to it. The same features that gave birth to Lockport in the early nineteenth century could be employed to help revive the local economy at the turn of the twenty-first century. And history would provide the guiding light.

Examining some sources from the recent past produces feelings of optimism or pessimism, depending upon when one reads them and assesses the situation of contemporary Lockport at that point in time. For example, in the special centennial issue of the *Union-Sun & Journal* published in July of 1965, an editorial on "The

100th Milestone" read: "The Erie Canal—once the lifeblood of Lockport's travel, industry and commerce—is now little more than a symbol on the city's insignia—a hallowed memory of a bygone day. Industries which flourished 100 years ago are relegated today to the yellowed pages of history." This rather somber observation also cautioned against speculating on what the future might bring, beyond acknowledging the certainty of "great change." The editors also paid faithful homage and offered a debt of gratitude to the pioneers of the old days, wondering whether their spirit might not offer some strength to face the unknown:

> Today as we pause to honor the memory of the city's founders, we can only resolve to meet the challenges of our own day with the same courage, determination and spirit of fairness and unselfishness with which they met theirs.

Read from the perspective of hindsight, one can lament the fact that there was not a better appreciation of what the "yellowed pages of history" might have offered in terms of restoring the canal to a more prominent place in the city's economy, and the pitfalls of ignoring its potential as a tourist attraction for so long—especially in light of the lost years and missed opportunities during the 1970s and 1980s.

Another helpful source, though off the beaten path, is a dissertation written by a student of architecture at Cornell University in 1976: "The Effect of the Erie Canal on Building and Planning in Syracuse, Palmyra, Rochester and Lockport, New York." The author, Vivienne Maddox, wanted to examine the consequences of the "decline and abandonment" of the canal on community life, and her work as a whole makes a good case for the importance of historic preservation efforts in these canal towns. Her central thesis—that the Erie Canal has always functioned as a catalyst—is especially relevant to Lockport.

Dr. Maddox demonstrated a fine appreciation of history in her writing. Quoting Rochester historian Blake McKelvey's article "The Erie Canal: Mother of Cities," she noted that it was in Lockport where "Mother Erie achieved immaculate conception." The city had previously expressed "faith that the enlarged canal would bring renewed prosperity," and that faith was needed again. In decades past, the canal at Lockport had been able to "cast a spell" on visitors to the locks: "The effect of the glimmering light between the black stone walls was like magic. No traveler should visit Lockport without witnessing such a scene." Perhaps what was needed was a renewal of the spirit of "the wisdom and boldness of the original projectors" of the locks, for the work of recovering that spirit might overcome the sense of melancholy and upheaval apparent during the 1970s. She concluded her study with some sound advice for those wishing to revive the canal towns: "It will be necessary to present the visual proof of this past force which was so powerful in shaping the present. *Preserving the heritage is essential.*"

During the past decade or so, several initiatives have been pursued in Lockport and along the canal corridor that have taken this advice to heart. There have been starts and stops along the way, some of them stemming from the lack of government funds, but there are promising indications that the tide is turning in a positive direction, as a result of a combination of these efforts. The Western Erie Canal Heritage Corridor Planning Commission stalled when "Albany turned off the money spigot," to the chagrin of local politicians and citizens. Private efforts, combined with some government support, have been more successful at picking up the slack, and that renaissance in Lockport is coming to fruition. A regular stream of articles in the local newspapers since 2002 have focused on "Cashing in on the canal—Waterway creating a stream of revenue." In the July 14 Sunday edition of the *Union-Sun,* Charles Richardson reported on the multiplicity of recreational opportunities available along the canal—"a stark contrast to just a few years ago, when the Erie Canal system was considered by some a deteriorating nuisance." In true pioneering sprit, Mike Murphy started his canal cruise business in 1987, and it has become a "brilliant success on the banks of the canal." John D'Onofrio recalled that the first few years were rough, but the enterprise of "Lockport Locks and Erie Canal Cruises" located on historic Market Street, had emerged as one of "the most attractive, well-managed and classy establishments along the canal," and includes the Canalside restaurant and banquet room, a gift shop, and a museum: "Murphy has completely re-written local history books and linked his name forever alongside other successful Erie Barge Canal entrepreneurs of the past like DeWitt Clinton or Birdsill Holly." This gem of Lockport tourism has dovetailed with the increased presence of the Lockport Cave and Underground Boat Ride, which takes visitors on a tour of the water power/hydraulic tunnel "blasted out of solid rock in the 1800s." Also, the Historic Towpath Trolley provides a tour around the streets of the city, with a narrator pointing out famous spots and telling stories that highlight Lockport's history.

A spirit of recovery and revival is also apparent at other locations around the city. The Kenan Center continues to serve as the city's center for culture and the arts, and the Market Street Art Center, housing a collection of galleries and studios, recently opened in a building across from Murphy's Erie Canal Boat Cruises establishment. A real community effort was involved in the re-opening of the Historic Palace Theatre on East Avenue, which functions not only as a classic movie theatre today, but also provides a stage for local theatrical productions and occasional concerts. The grand old theatre was built in 1925 under the direction of the stage manager of the Hodge Opera House, so it provides a real link to the past. In its heyday, Lockport could boast of a multitude of theatres, including the Hodge Opera House, the Hi-Art, and the Rialto. The Palace is the only one to survive, in most of its original splendor, proof of Lockport's renewed community spirit and interest in preserving its heritage.

The last piece of the Lockport effort to rescue the past and redeem the future is the Erie Canal Discovery Center, which opened in June of 2005 after years of cooperative and exemplary effort by the Niagara County Historical Society, the city, and the Presbyterian Church, assisted by a grant from the Grigg-Lewis Trust, and other funding sources secured with the help of local state and federal representatives. The interactive museum is located in the Hamilton House, "a deteriorating 19th century structure near the canal" recognized for its value by a "few men of vision." Foremost among them was David Dickinson, Niagara County historian, who died before he could see this dream come true. The historic landmark building was "saved from the wrecking ball, an unfortunate fate common to most of the historic structures that once lined Main Street in Lockport." It is a most fitting place for such a museum, as the building has been a mainstay in the city's history, changing with the times. It was originally built as the Universalist Church, and transformed by the Presbyterian Church into a youth recreational and community outreach center. To reclaim and celebrate Lockport's history, as a spark to the city's growing tourism business, shows a stroke of ingenuity that would have made the greats of the nineteenth century proud.

A replica of the Raphael Beck mural is the focal point of the museum, key to "the interpretive mission of the Erie Canal Discovery Center—explaining the role that Lockport played in the opening of the Erie Canal." The center also features an interactive packet boat trip on the *Western Comet*, as well as computer kiosks that highlight people from Lockport's past—all in an effort to bring Lockport's past to life again, for both its residents and tourists. It is a crowning achievement in the renaissance currently underway in Historic Lockport.

Voices from the past echo today, across the decades and even the centuries, at this time of renewed hope in Lockport: Clarence Lewis, sounding the refrain of the importance of historic preservation during the 17 years he wrote his historical vignette columns for the local newspaper, and historians and writers whose subject was the Erie Canal. Their words resonate with a special poignancy today, whether coming from George Condon, who noted in *Stars in the Water* "how thoroughly the Erie Canal and its complex lock installation are interwoven in every fiber of this picturesque city," or *Erie Water*, a 1933 novel written by Walter D. Edmonds and quoted in *Low Bridge! Folklore and the Erie Canal*:

> They walked down to the Deep Cut, and they saw that the canal was more than half full . . . [the water] made a dark, straight track along the towpath wall, stretching back into the still blackness of the stone. But even in that blackness, it held reflections of the stars.

Traveling back further in time, the words of Tocqueville on the "canal craze" are heard anew, as he wrote of how Americans changed the whole order of nature to their advantage—"they found their future by floating into it"—just as Lockport is "sailing uphill" into the future by reclaiming the legacy of the canal. From its genesis the Erie Canal has functioned as a catalyst, and "a symbol of the enduring yet adaptable quality of human technology and ingenuity," according to the History Channel's *Modern Marvels* program. "Founded at nearly the beginning of the American republic, it is still going strong today"—which is certainly true in Lockport.

Numerous chroniclers of Lockport's history spoke of the fortuitous circumstances that led to its rise, and it is hoped that good fortune has returned—along with a bit of the romance and magic that was often recognized in the past. A display in the new Erie Canal Discovery Center features a quote by Francis Kimball that captures this sense of magic: "The Erie Canal rubbed Aladdin's lamp. America awoke, catching for the first time this wondrous vision of its own dimensions and power."

From the earliest days, when the idea first took hold of Jesse Hawley, the canal has been a source of inspiration and renewed confidence. Hawley would follow his star and settle in Lockport, which was beginning to establish its reputation as the historic jewel of the Erie Canal. Today's determination to reclaim and honor that historic legacy is conjuring up a revived community spirit in the Lock City that Jesse Hawley would have applauded. New hope has been found in the history of the place where the earthly remains—and spirit—of the man with the vision rest in the shade trees of Lockport's Cold Springs Cemetery.

BIBLIOGRAPHY

In addition to the standard list of works consulted, a brief summary of the most important resources I used is in order.

My major source of information on Lockport's history was the rich treasure-trove at the local history room of the Lockport Public Library. The files of articles by Clarence Lewis (compiled and indexed by Christa Caldwell) were invaluable as an introduction to major people and events of Lockport's past. A detailed chronology put together by Christopher W. Speck in 1989 was a frequently consulted source, as I scanned it repeatedly for context and to double check facts and dates. Numerous commemorative booklets preserved over the years by wise librarians were also a great help, as were the surviving newspaper sources from Lockport, Lewiston, Rochester, and Buffalo. In addition to the bound copies of *Priestcraft Exposed and Primitive Christianity Defended* at the Niagara County Historian's Office, my insights on Lyman Spalding were also formed by reviewing some of the letters sent to me by the librarians at the Division of Rare and Manuscript Collections at Cornell University.

Three monographs on the Erie Canal were another major source of information and inspiration—as each one in turn demonstrated an appreciation of the importance of Lockport's role in the story of the canal, and set a high standard for any historian writing about the canal and the towns it spawned: George E. Condon's *Stars in the Water* (1974), Carol Sheriff's *The Artificial River* (1996), and Peter L. Bernstein's *Wedding of the Waters* (2005). I cannot imagine being able to write my book without these sources, and I know I would not have enjoyed the work as much without them as steady and reliable guides.

Books, Articles, Pamphlets, and other Unpublished Works

Amato, Joseph. *Rethinking Home: A Case for Writing Local History*. Berkeley, California: University of California Press, 2002.

Andrist, Ralph K. *The Erie Canal*. New York: American Heritage Publishing Co., 1964.

Berton, Pierre. *Niagara: A History of the Falls*. New York: Penguin Putnam Inc., 1992.

Bernstein, Peter L. *Wedding of the Waters: The Erie Canal and the Making of a Great Nation*. New York: W. W. Norton & Co., 2005.

Billington, Ray Allen. *The Protestant Crusade, 1800–1860: A Study of the Origins of American Nativism*. New York: Macmillan, 1938.

Bourne, Russell. *Floating West: The Erie and Other American Canals*. New York: W. W. Norton & Co., 1992.

Brooks, Charles E. *Frontier Settlement and Market Revolution: The Holland Land Purchase*. Ithaca: Cornell University Press, 1996.

Condon, George E. *Stars in the Water: The Story of the Erie Canal*. Garden City, New York: Doubleday and Company, 1974.

Cornog, Evan. *The Birth of Empire: DeWitt Clinton and the American Experience, 1769–1828*. New York: Oxford University Press, 1998.

Cross, Whitney R. *The Burned-over District: The Social and Intellectual History of Enthusiastic Religion in Western New York, 1800–1850*. Ithaca: Cornell University Press, 1950.

Cuming. F. H. "An Address, Delivered at the Laying of the Cap-Stone, of the Ten Combined Locks at Lockport, on the Anniversary of St. John the Baptist, June 24, 1825." Lockport: Orsamus Turner, 1825.

Davis, David Brion. "Some Themes of Counter-Subversion: An Analysis of Anti-Masonic, Anti-Catholic and Anti-Mormon Literature." *Mississippi Valley Historical Review* 47, 205–224: 1960.

Dolan, Jay P. *The American Catholic Parish (Vol. I)*. New York: Paulist Press, 1987.

Donohue, Rev. Thomas. *History of the Catholic Church in Western New York: Diocese of Buffalo*. Buffalo: Catholic Historical Publishing Company, 1904.

Dumphrey, OSFS, Rev. Joseph. "The History of Catholics in Lockport, New York." presentation at St. John the Baptist Church, August 3, 2004.

Ellis, David M. et al. *A Short History of New York State*. Ithaca: Cornell University Press, 1967.

Frederickson, Madelyn P. "The Life and Times of Birdsill Holly." Lockport: Blue Spruce Publishing, 1996.

Harkness, Cheryl. *The Amazing Impossible Erie Canal*. New York: Simon & Schuster Books for Young Readers, 1995.

Haydon, Roger, editor. *Upstate Travels: British Views of Nineteenth Century New York*. Syracuse: Syracuse University Press, 1982.

History of Niagara County, New York with illustrations descriptive of its scenery, private residences, public buildings, fine blocks and important manufactures. New York: Sanford & Co., Press of George McNamara, 1878.

Johnson, Paul E. *A Shopkeeper's Millennium: Society and Revivals in Rochester, New York, 1815–1837*. New York: Hill & Wang, 1978.

Kammen, Carol. *On Doing Local History: Reflections on What Local Historians Do, Why, and What It Means*. London: Alta Mira Press, 1995.

Klein, Milton M., editor. *The Empire State: A History of New York*. Ithaca: Cornell University Press; Cooperstown: New York State Historical Association, 2001.

Lewis, Clarence O. "Synopsis of the History of Lockport, New York," Lockport: Niagara County Court House, 1962.

——————. "The Erie Canal, 1817–1967, Occasional Contributions of the Niagara County Historical Society." Lockport: 1967.

——————. "The Morgan Affair." Lockport: Niagara County Court House, 1966.

Maddox, Vivienne Dawn. "The Effect of the Erie Canal on Building and Planning in Syracuse, Palmyra, Rochester, and Lockport, New York." Ph.D. dissertation: Cornell University, 1976.

McGreevy, Patrick. *Imagining Niagara: The Meaning and Making of Niagara Falls.* Amherst, Massachusetts: University of Massachusetts Press, 1994.

Morris, Jeffrey B. and Richard B. Morris, editors. *Encyclopedia of American History.* New York: Harper Collins Publishers, 1996.

Muller Jr., Alexis. *Looking Back so that we may move ahead: 150th Anniversary of the Grand Erie Canal.* Lockport: 1975.

Murphy, Cait and Rosanne Haggerty. "The Erie Rising." *American Heritage* 53, 62–71: 2001.

Oates, Joyce Carol. "My Father, My Fiction," *New York Times Magazine.* March 16, 1989.

——————. *Wonderland.* Princeton: Ontario Review Press, 1971.

Rapp, Marvin A. *Canal Water and Whiskey: Tall Tales from the Erie Canal Country.* Buffalo: Western New York Heritage Institute Press, 1992.

Reed, I. Richard. "Evolutionary History of Niagara County, New York." Lockport: 1978.

Rhodes, Lynwood Mark. "How They Built the Erie." *American Vistas.* New York: Oxford University Press, 1975.

Seelye, John. "Rational Exultation: The Erie Canal Celebration." *Proceedings of the American Antiquarian Society* 94, 241–267: 1984.

Shaw, Ronald E. *Erie Water West: A History of the Erie Canal, 1792–1854.* Lexington, Kentucky: University of Kentucky Press, 1966.

Sheriff, Carol. *The Artificial River: The Erie Canal and the Paradox of Progress, 1817–1862.* New York: Hill & Wang, 1996.

Smith, Aunt Ednah. "Recollections of an Old Settler." Niagara County Historical Society. 1897.

"Souvenir History of Niagara County: Commemorative of the 25th Anniversary of Pioneer Association of Niagara County." 1902.

"Souvenir Program Commemorating the Lockport Centennial. Niagara County, New York, 1865–1965."

Spalding, Lyman A. "Recollections of the War of 1812 and Early Life in Western New York, Occasional Contributions of the Niagara County Historical Society." Lockport:1949.

Speck, Christopher W. "A Brief History of Lockport and its Environs." 1989.

Strauss, Gertrude. "Our First Hundred and Fifty Years." Lockport: First Presbyterian Church of Lockport, 1973.

"To Commemorate the 125th Anniversary Church of St. Patrick's Parish, Lockport, New York and the Golden Jubilee of Ordination of Its Pastor Msgr. McCarthy, June 3, 1989."

Tocqueville, Alexis De. *Democracy in America.* New York: Alfred A. Knopf, 1980.

Trollope, Frances. *Domestic Manners of the Americans*. St. James, New York: Brandywine Press, 1993.

Turner, Orsamus. *Pioneer History of the Holland Purchase of Western New York*. Buffalo: George H. Derby & Co, 1850.

Tyler, Alice Felt. *Freedom's Ferment: Phases of American Social History from the Colonial Period to the Outbreak of the Civil War*. New York: Harper and Brothers, 1962.

Walker, Barbara K. and Warren S., editors. *The Erie Canal: Gateway to Empire*. Boston: D. C. Heath, 1963.

Way, Peter. *Common Labor: Workers and the Digging of North American Canals, 1780–1860*. Baltimore: Johns Hopkins University Press, 1993.

Wilber, Joshua. "Lockport Old Home Week Souvenir, 1910."

Wilner, Merton M. *Niagara Frontier: A Narrative and Documentary History*. Chicago: The S. J. Clarke Publishing Co., 1931.

Wyld, Lionel D. *Low Bridge! Folklore and the Erie Canal*. Syracuse: Syracuse University Press, 1962.

Videos

"The Erie Canal." *Modern Marvels* series. The History Channel, 2000.

"Our Town: Lockport." WNED-TV, Buffalo, 2004.

Online Resources

http://www.elockport.com

http://history.rochester.edu/canal

Hosack, David. "Memoir of DeWitt Clinton: With an Appendix, Containing Numerous Documents, Illustrative of the Principal Events of His Life." 1829

Stone, William L. "Narrative of the Festivities Observed in Honor of the Completion of the Grand Erie Canal Uniting the Waters of the Great Western Lakes with the Atlantic Ocean." 1825.

Whitford, Noble E. "History of the Canal System of the State of New York Together with Brief Histories of the Canals of the United States and Canada." 1905.

http://www.lockport-ny.com/History

http://www.niagara-county.org

http://xroad.virginia.edu

Hawley, Jesse. *Hercules Essays*.

INDEX

Ancient Order of Hibernians, 90, 117, 138

Anti-Masonic Party, 55, 56, 63, 64, 98, 99, 100, 101

Barge Canal system, 79, 126, 127, 148, 150

Batavia, 26, 64, 97–99

Beck, A. Raphael, 91, 93, 136, 146, 151

Bernstein, Peter L., 30–33, 40, 47, 48

Big Bridge, 79, 80, 90, 92, 98, 117, 127

Bond, Colonel William, 27, 29, 30

Brown, Esek, 22, 24, 26, 27

Bruce, Eli, 43, 98, 100, 101

Buffalo, 11, 16, 20, 21, 23, 26, 32, 41, 44, 47–51, 56, 114, 115, 127–129, 134–138, 144–148

Canandaigua, 14, 29, 30, 52, 57, 97, 98, 100, 101

Carpenter, Benjamin, 129

Caverno, Sullivan, 118, 119

Clinton, De Witt, 16, 17, 20, 21, 23, 33, 40, 41–43, 46–48, 50, 56, 74, 78, 99, 100, 146, 150

Cold Springs Cemetery, 152

Colden, Cadwallader, 12, 13, 48, 49, 50, 51, 53

Comstock brothers, 22, 23, 24, 27, 30, 109, 113, 122

Condon, George E., 23, 31, 34, 36, 48, 49, 51, 130, 131, 134, 151

Cross, Whitney R., 56, 57, 58, 64, 105, 106, 107

Cuming, Rev. F. H., 46, 47, 98

Delphi-Harrison, 87, 140, 142

DeSales Catholic School, 83, 116, 118

Dibble, Orange, 35

Dickinson, David, 35, 151

Erie Canal Discovery Center, 92, 93, 150–152

First Presbyterian Church, 29, 92, 103, 106, 109–112, 147

Gaffney, Frank J., 136

Granchelli, Elmer, 143, 144

Haines, Jesse, 24, 27, 66

Harrison, Herbert Champion, 87, 139, 141, 145

Harrison Radiator, 138, 140, 142

Hawley, Jesse, 14–18, 20, 27, 48, 94, 125, 152

Hercules essays, 13–18, 48, 72

Hodge Opera House, 77, 132, 137, 138, 150

Holland Land Purchase, 13, 19, 104

Holly, Birdsill, 78, 130–134, 137, 145, 150

Holly Manufacturing Co., 131–134, 137, 141

Hydraulic Raceway/Power Co., 124

Hudson River, 12, 13, 15, 17, 22, 42, 47

Hunt, Washington, 75, 89, 112, 119, 124, 127, 131, 133, 141, 145

Irish immigrants, 22, 25, 26, 33, 35–40, 52, 57, 59, 90, 104, 108, 109, 114–117, 121

Jefferson, Thomas, 13, 15, 43, 138

Kenan, William Rand, 146–147

Kenan Center, 94, 147, 150

Kinyon, David R., 142–144

Lafayette, Marquis de, 11, 43–46, 130

Lockport Locks and Erie Canal Cruises, 85, 150

Lockport-Niagara Falls Strap Railway, 126

Lake Ontario, 11, 14, 19, 136

Lake Erie, 11, 12, 14, 15, 19, 22, 44, 47, 50

Lewis, Clarence O., 21, 26, 34, 38, 39, 45, 64, 97, 98, 100, 101, 103, 105, 108, 116, 118, 119, 123–125, 127, 128, 135–138, 141, 151

Lewiston, 13, 20, 24, 26, 28, 29, 38, 39, 44, 97, 98, 99, 102, 109, 118, 130

Lockport Observatory, 19, 28, 35, 50, 130

Lockport Public Library, 55, 56, 119, 141

Lockport Union Sun & Journal, 105, 130

Lockwood, Belva, 146

Lowertown, 24, 74, 82, 83, 111, 112, 116, 117, 128, 131, 141, 142

Main Street, 24, 25, 28, 30, 77, 89, 90, 91, 118, 124, 127, 136, 142, 143, 144, 145, 151

Market Strret, 24, 77, 117, 124, 131, 132, 137, 142, 150

Marsh, O. C., 146

Masons, 29, 40, 44, 46, 47, 55, 56, 57, 63, 64, 97–102, 109, 118, 119

McCollum, Joel, 55, 111, 114

McLeod, Alexander, 74, 102–103, 135

Merchant, George, 130, 131

Merchant's Gargling Oil, 131, 132, 137, 138

Miller, William E., 88, 147

Morgan, William H., 29, 55, 63–64, 74, 97–101, 135

Morris, Gouverneur, 12, 14, 30

Morris, Robert, 13, 19

Muller, Alexis Jr., 121, 123, 126

Niagara Falls, 11, 14, 44, 51, 52, 102, 126, 127, 132, 134, 137, 147

Niagara County, 11, 13, 16, 19, 20, 27, 28, 29, 55, 60, 64, 65, 72, 75, 76, 77, 98, 100, 101, 103, 105, 107, 108, 111, 113, 119, 120, 122, 123, 124, 125, 126, 128, 129, 130, 135, 142, 143, 146

Niagara County Hist. Society, 25, 27, 69, 90, 138, 150

Niagara River, 11, 13, 14, 102

Oates, Joyce Carol, 88, 147–148

Old Home Week, 21, 120, 121, 139

Palace Theatre, 84, 138, 150

Patriot War, 74, 102–103

Pioneer Line, 60–62

Pound, John, 29, 30, 119

Priestcraft Exposed and Primitive Christianity Defended, 57–63

Quakers, 22, 27, 29, 57–59, 62, 72, 104, 105, 108, 109, 113

Ridge Road, 20, 72, 83, 98

Roberts, Nathan S., 25, 33–36, 46

Rochester, 20, 33, 37, 38, 40, 45, 46, 50, 52, 53, 56, 61, 62, 64, 98, 105, 106, 107, 114, 127, 129, 136, 149

Sabbatarianism, 57, 60, 61

Sheriff, Carol, 12, 15, 23, 45, 100, 107, 119, 122, 123, 124, 125

Smith, Dr. Isaac, 25, 27, 28, 30

Smith, "Aunt" Ednah, 25, 30, 36, 37, 65, 92

Spalding, Lyman A., 19, 23, 29, 30, 43, 55, 57–63, 65, 92, 108, 111, 114, 119, 121–124, 128–130, 145

St. John's Church, 71, 114–117

St. Patrick's Church, 36, 70, 71, 104, 116, 117

Stone, William L., 41, 48, 49, 50

Tocqueville, Alexis de, 51, 54, 56, 104, 151

Towpath Trolley, 150

Transit Street/Road, 20, 94, 109, 136

Trollope, Frances, 31, 51, 52, 53, 102

Tucker, Morris, 26, 131, 132, 144

Turner, Orsamus, 19, 24, 28, 30, 46, 100, 101, 104, 127, 130

Ulrich, David, 144, 145

Union School, 30, 73, 118, 119, 146

Union Station, 136, 145

Upson, Charles A., 139, 141

Upson Company, 138, 140, 141

War of 1812, 16, 20, 50, 57, 102

Washington House, 28, 29, 44, 50, 100, 130, 137

Wedding of the Waters, 30, 31, 40, 41, 47, 48

Weed, Thurlow, 53, 98

Whitford, Noble, 32, 33

Widewater's Marina, 86, 142

Wilber, Joshua, 121, 127, 131

Wright's Corners, 29, 101

Wyndham Lawn Home, 89, 146